PENGUIN REFERENCE BOOKS

CYBERSEARCH

From the first days of computer-based information retrieval to the recent explosion of Internet applications, John A. Butler worked in IBM marketing, management training, and technical education. His articles on computer technology have been published by Macmillan-McGraw Hill, Science Research Associates, LAN Technology, and Capital PC Monitor. He is the author of *Computers and Communications, Strike Able-Peter: The Stranding and Salvage of the USS* Missouri, and *Sailing on Friday: The Perilous Voyage of America's Merchant Marine*. He holds degrees in Nautical Science from the Massachusetts Maritime Academy and in Physics from Holy Cross College. In his spare time he manages the Web site of the Massachusetts Maritime Academy Alumni Association.

John A. Butler [23]

CyberSearch

Research Techniques in
the Electronic Age

PENGUIN REFERENCE

PENGUIN REFERENCE
Published by the Penguin Group
Penguin Putnam Inc., 375 Hudson Street,
New York, New York 10014, U.S.A.
Penguin Books Ltd, 27 Wrights Lane,
London W8 5TZ, England
Penguin Books Australia Ltd, Ringwood,
Victoria, Australia
Penguin Books Canada Ltd, 10 Alcorn Avenue,
Toronto, Ontario, Canada M4V 3B2
Penguin Books (N.Z.) Ltd, 182–190 Wairau Road,
Auckland 10, New Zealand
Penguin India, 210 Chiranjiv Tower, 43 Nehru Place,
New Delhi, India 11009

Penguin Books Ltd, Registered Offices:
Harmondsworth, Middlesex, England

First published in Penguin Reference 1998

1 3 5 7 9 10 8 6 4 2

A NOTE TO THE READER
The information in this book is provided as is with no express or implied warranties. While every effort has been made to ensure the accuracy of information, the author and publisher assume no responsibility for errors or omissions, or for damages resulting from the use of the information contained herein.

Grateful acknowledgment is made to the following organizations for permission to reproduce screens captured in online searches: Colorado Alliance of Research Libraries; Lycos Inc.; Montgomery County (Maryland) Department of Public Libraries; The UnCover Company; Usenet Inc.; and Yahoo Inc.

LIBRARY OF CONGRESS CATALOGING IN PUBLICATION DATA
Butler, John A.
    CyberSearch: research techniques in the electronic age/John A. Butler.
    p.   cm.
    Includes bibliographical references (p.   ) and index.
    ISBN 0 14 05.1387 6 (pbk.)
    1. Information retrieval—United States.   2. Libraries—United States.   I. Title.
    ZA3075.888   1998
    025.5´24—dc21   97–44756

Printed in the United States of America
Set in ITC Garamond
Designed by Kate Nichols

For Allison

Acknowledgments

The information in this book is provided as is with no express or implied warranties. While every effort has been made to ensure the accuracy of information, the author and/or publisher assume no responsibility for errors or omissions, or for damages resulting from the use of the information contained herein.

The author and publisher are grateful to the following organizations for permission to reproduce screens captured in online searches:

Colorado Alliance of Research Libraries
Lycos Inc.
Montgomery County (Maryland) Department of Public
    Libraries
The UnCover Company
Usenet Inc.
Yahoo! Inc.

Contents

Introduction

Travel with me to Cambridge, Massachusetts, and stand near the north bank of the Charles River. Across the water you can see the red brick buildings of the Harvard Business School. The major campus of Harvard University is behind you, where you can find the Widener Library and the Schools of Government, Law and Divinity. All are within walking distance, near or just beyond Harvard Square, but this is only the beginning.

Downstream, the sprawling complex of MIT is worthy of a visit. Nearby is Boston's Museum of Science. The Harvard Medical School is across the river, as are the offices of *The New England Journal of Medicine* and *The Atlantic Monthly*. There's no telling what you'll hear near the New England Conservatory of Music. A short trip on the MTA brings you to the campus of Boston University and as well as those of several other universities, and museums, galleries, and libraries. You have been given a special passcard allowing free access to all these facilities. It permits you to browse libraries, take classes, attend lectures, and consult with faculty and staff. Access to information within that august array of intelligence is yours, just by using the passcard. Imagine that you want to test it, but nothing tells you how it works. What do you do next?

That is why you have me along.

This book is about gathering information. I have written it for students, teachers, historians, journalists, novelists, amateur and professional writers—just about any curious person. Writers always have a need for facts, their interest hardly limited to nonfiction. Authors are constantly seeking backgrounds for short stories and novels. Even poetry requires realistic references to draw the reader into the narrator's company. Whatever your motivation, you should find new ideas here, tips, techniques, plans and actions to help you get the best return for your research efforts.

You can visit not only Cambridge and Boston, but Berkeley, Minneapolis, Washington, D.C., even overseas, and you can do it electronically without leaving home. You'll need access to a modem-equipped personal computer and should know how to poke through disk directory structures, print, copy, and edit files, activities like that—enough to use a word processor, care for your data and connect to a remote computer.

Hunting for facts is like mining for gems—lots of time spent, much of it on empty veins, before unearthing real treasure. You could easily devote a third of your time on a writing project to research. The activity doesn't end even when your writing nears completion. Research can be a heavy investment in time and perhaps in money, and few researchers get paid directly for their efforts, so it's important to make the time productive.

A scholarly piece of nonfiction reflects immense research

effort. *Truman*, David McCullough's 992-page biography of the mid-century president averages one citation per page. His bibliography runs for twenty-five pages of small print. James McPherson's *Battle Cry of Freedom* includes eighteen pages of bibliographic notes. Each of twenty-eight chapters contains dozens of footnotes, on practically every one of 862 pages.

Research time can lengthen or shorten the creative process. My purpose is to work with you to make that phase of your creative efforts pay off. The tips and techniques provided are based on my own experience, with much help from the referenced texts. New information technology and the widely discussed information highway caused me to collect and document details on modern research methods. The computer systems I use here for illustration reflect no bias on my part; they are widely available, and I found them to be straightforward—a good way to get started. I tried to put what I learned into practice, to prove the content of what I was writing about. Along the way, I compiled lists of useful sources and stashed words and acronyms into a glossary. If I can give you a few useful references and some fresh ideas to enhance your research efforts, in effect explain how to use that magic passcard, possibly to reduce the time between the idea and its written description, then I've accomplished my purpose. Enjoy the trip!

John A. Butler
jabutler@cpcug.org

CyberSearch

I

Net Ready

The Internet

The place to gather the latest information on everything from news to buying a car is on the Internet. Before we can begin to surf the Net, let's clear up some myths.

Internet Mythology

Myth One: *The Internet is free.* Many people don't realize that e-mail, therefore most electronic research, has a price in access or connect-time fees. Somebody has to pay for the computers and telephone lines, through tuition, taxes, or direct fees. Unless you are on a university, government, or business network, to use the Internet you will need to connect through an online service or an independent service provider (ISP). Internet service providers charge a monthly fee (in 1997, $19.95 was a typical introductory price) for a basic amount of connect-time. Any time over that is separately billed. Fees vary according to the services offered, and the means of access. Services (Internet applications) are described in chapter 5. A guide to service providers is in Appendix A. Subscribers to Internet service providers pay a monthly membership fee and sometimes are offered unlimited use of Internet without additional hourly fees. Currently, the major online services are CompuServe, Microsoft, and America Online (AOL) and are quite suitable for casual Net connections. For moderate to heavy use, say fifteen to twenty hours per month or more, it would be worth your while to go with an Internet service provider as it would cost less per unit of time to be connected to the network. The technique that's best for you, whether through an online service or by a subscription to an Internet service provider, depends on the facilities you use, what extent you use them, and how often. In comparing the two approaches, the break-even point is an elusive and moving target, one found only by experimentation. If you already subscribe to an online service, that is all you need to get started.

Myth Two: *The Internet is costly.* It isn't free, but neither is it costly. You may already be using it without being aware. A survey done by the National Commission on Libraries and Information Science by Charles McClure and colleagues found public libraries went from providing 13 percent of public access to the Internet in 1994, to 28 percent in 1996, and to a projected 50 percent by March 1997.[1] If the terminals in your library allow access to the catalogs of other libraries, chances are that connections exist "under the covers" through an Internet client-server arrangement. In chapter 4 we illustrate a system used by many public libraries as an example of online bibliographic research. Part of that process takes place by telnet connections (a telephone connection to another computer) providing access to remote computer systems. Such access is usually restricted to community residents with library cards. It is their taxes (or tuition, on campus) that support the library and its telephone lines. Although this type of use is confined to catalog searching, it could be the most common application a writer would make of online facilities. Another common information research application consists of the searching mechanisms on the World Wide Web. As you will learn in chapter 5, advertising increasingly pays for that.

Myth Three: *The Internet saves time.* For most people the Internet is a time-waster until they learn to use it wisely, disciplining themselves to specific purposes. Internet "newsgroups," electronic bulletin boards in which people trade comments within defined topics, may be rich sources of expertise. But there exists what Net users call a high signal-to-noise ratio, useful discussions buried within a lot of idle chatter. The forums or conferences in commercial services are no different. Occasionally you will find a forum or newsgroup with just the information you seek. However open discussions tend to lose focus, often straying from the topic while maintaining the original subject and purpose of the thread. (A thread is a series of sequentially connected postings on a subject identified in the message headers, a more-or-less lucid conversation among two or more people.) I can't recall how often I have patiently tracked a thread, flipping through thank-you notes, trivial comments, typo-corrections, asides, even messages that have nothing to do with the original subject, looking for just one gem of wisdom on the original topic. That time-wasting condition reflects on the overseer of the newsgroup or conference, someone who can interrupt the thread and issue a gentle reminder to take such commentary elsewhere. Irrelevant material often goes unpurged because it keeps electronically friendly people associated. Sometimes there is truly no one in charge. This approach, while costing little in money, does cost in time and patience.

Hundreds of computers directly connected on the Internet support special interest groups, professional organizations, university departments, databases, and electronic mailing lists, called "listservs." Some newsgroups are monitored and contain less chaff, although the topics within broad categories may be quite diverse. Another major problem with popular newsgroups is that some are so popular that they may be unable to sustain peak-hour demand. Then, latecomers get a cold "not available" message, as if the facility had gone out of operation. That means attempting to re-access at an off-peak time, lengthening your work day, or at least requiring adjusted hours. Serious, speedy research can be done on the Net late at night.

Myth Four: *Internet expertise is unlimited.* There is substance to this myth, but be wary. Thousands of academics do use it every day. It's heavily installed in government and universities. Defining the size of the Net is like counting raindrops over a given area. Several surveys have been made, some contested as being statistically invalid, but no one really knows how many people use it regularly. A study made by Andrew Kohut and Associates in the fall of 1995 for the Times-Mirror Company has been referenced often by newspaper columnists. Another, the American Internet User Survey, conducted during the same period by Emerging Technologies Research Group, tended to support the same broad figures: somewhere between 8 and 10 million American adults were then regular users. A survey released in May 1997, reported that use of the Internet quadrupled in the past three years to more than 30 million users.[2] Whatever the number of users today, that figure is certain to be larger tomorrow.

The same growth could be said for Internet resources. Scores of Web sites offer access to "search engines" that convert submitted key words to lists of Internet resources. Before Carnegie Mellon's Lycos, a popular search engine on the Web, went commercial in 1995, its index listed over 3 million Internet resources, and Lycos confidently predicted that its commercial operation would soon exceed 6 million entries. While topics found across the Net are wide-ranging, most tend to be introductory. Many items, if converted to the printed page, would be considered flyers or brochures for the detailed sources of information.

Some of the most knowledgeable people in the academic and scientific fields don't participate in online activity. Some librarians who know their way around the stacks and have memorized the pathways through the reference shelves are outright technophobes. Fear of "crashing the system," chimera that it is, lurks under the bed. Nor do all archivists and museum curators hang out on the Net. They have more demands on their time. How will you get to those people and get the information you need?

Even when you do find a newsgroup with apparently useful material, you have no assurance of a correspondent's authority because of e-mail's inherent anonymity. Many people don't cite their credentials. Besides, anyone can pose as an expert. The best information you can get initially is apt to be a reference to something of which you were not aware but can then investigate for yourself. Internet newsgroups can be valuable for that alone. I have been directed to software problem solutions, owners of out-of-print books, and to important people who know nothing about communicating through electronic communities. But I wouldn't expect to get more in the way of reliable legal, medical, or investment advice on the Net than I could find in my public library. It is best to start with the assumption that you are conversing with peers, people who know things that you don't, while you probably know things that they don't. Gradually, by trading information, you develop some virtual relationships and can assess the relative validity of your sources. Meanwhile you will probably have learned a few things along the way.

A great way to specialize on the Net is through subscriptions to mailing lists, or listservs. A listserv is a group of people specifically focused on a subject of mutual interest. This, too, has its shortcomings. Newsgroups differ from mailing lists in the same way that public bulletin boards differ from magazine subscriptions. You can ignore newsgroups or read them at leisure, but the files associated with mailing lists arrive faithfully and frequently in your electronic mailbox. A mailing list distribution might be large, and once your name is on the list, every time you log in you will receive all the mail generated since your last log in, sometimes including lengthy documents. All of this is stored in the data space your Internet service provider allocated to you on the Internet computer before being transferred to your hard disk; like your own disk, it can fill easily if not regularly purged. Some mailing lists require approval of an application before enrollment, possibly to separate the idle curious from the dedicated. A few require a subscription fee. You might spend more time reading and purging mail, but you should find that subscribers do tend to follow the topic, probably because they have more demanding interests. Also, many identify themselves with campus or professional addresses, lending a degree of authenticity to their correspondence. This could be a reliable way to identify subject matter authorities.

Despite the negative aspects of the Internet, even with its

frustrations it pays off for most researchers and is worth the time and expense to use it. Familiarity comes with use, and once you conquer the learning curve you could find many treasures behind your computer screen. It might take a few months in a well-disciplined, step-by-step approach to find and work comfortably with the useful channels of information on the Net, time that could yield rewarding results.

Technical Details: Your Internet Connection

(This section can be skipped if you have no interest in the technical aspects.)

Internet activity has a language all its own with terms that seem intended only for use by those in the know. I'll use a few in the following explanation, but don't be discouraged. Every term will be explained. Join me, and become one of the cognoscenti.

The Internet has been defined as a network of networks. These are connected on a "backbone" network originally funded by the Advanced Research Project Agency (ARPA) and the National Science Foundation (NSF). During its development, which started over twenty years ago, other public networks, some little more than bulletin board systems, began connecting to it. I include in my explanation of the Internet, any connected sub-network that has traffic passing both ways through a connecting gateway. Bitnet, shown as an example in Figure 1-1, is one such sub-network. The commercial on-line services offer gateway access to the Internet for many of its facilities. They are more properly considered peripheral to the Net than a part of it, but they constitute the single most popular Internet access method. In practical fact, we are all wired together, no matter what sub-network we might be as-

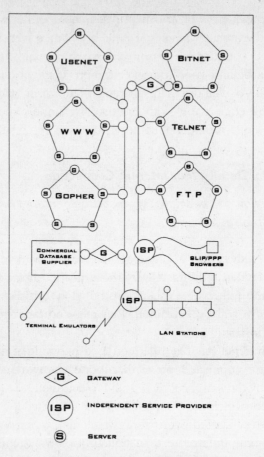

FIGURE 1-1   *Elements of the Internet*

sociated with. Any Internet service provider—including the commercial online services—offers perks to their customers, and special rates and charges for their services. Bear this in mind as you shop for the functions you need.

On campus or at work your computer may be connected to a LAN (local area network). If not, an emulator allows your computer to act like a combined keyboard and display at the end (hence "terminal") of a phone line, shoveling text-type information to and from the other end of the phone line one character at a time. Thus, faster is better. Image or sound transfers are a heavier load than terminal emulation programs can usually handle. Such transmission requires SLIP or PPP (Serial Line Internet Protocol/Point-to-Point Protocol) software in both your machine and the service provider's. Protocols manage the transmissions between your computer and the programs at the service provider. SLIP and PPP are separate protocols that do similar work; SLIP is older and better established, PPP more efficient. "Pseudo-SLIP" is an economical innovation offered by some service providers that emulates SLIP protocol between your computer and the service provider. Either SLIP, PPP, or pseudo-SLIP brings the Net's high speed packet switching, known as Transmission Control Protocol/Internetworking Protocol (TCP/IP), directly to the terminal, supporting transmission of large chunks of data on the best network route in well-labelled packets of data. For this, you need faster hardware on the lines, at least 9,600 bps, and a program to format and assemble or disassemble the contents of the packets for graphical presentation.

This alphabetic stuff is analagous to the protocols of regular telephone conversations that we all take for granted. When someone calls you, implied rules control the flow of human interaction. First, the phone company sends signals that ring your phone while producing a "ringing" sound at the caller's phone; when you pick up the handset, an exclusive link between you and the caller is established to support voice conversation on electrical circuits. We might call that Voice Protocol, or "VP." Next there is a mutual understanding between talkers that English will be spoken (confirmed by the opening "Hello"), while using certain courtesies (answering party speaks first, both warn of disconnection with words like "goodbye," voice inflections substitute for gestures, etc.). This we could call English Telephone Protocol, "ETP." ETP/VP for people then corresponds to TCP/IP for computers. You still can't transfer images until you have a video phone or fax machine on a separate line. That would need another set of rules, corresponding roughly to the protocols, SLIP or PPP. SLIP's major advantage is that it supports graphical data exchange and interaction with icons, using a mouse and pointer on a full-color screen.

After gaining some basic connection experience, you would find it helpful to take a course or read one or more current Internet textbooks. There are literally hundreds of books on Internet applications, with dozens more being published every month. Some of my favorites are listed in the Bibliography. In chapter 5 you will also learn how you may take a course *on* the Internet *via* the Internet itself.

From what we've said so far, you might feel that a simple e-mail account is not likely to be sufficient for your needs, but you also might feel that SLIP is too much for a beginner. SLIP's major shortcoming is the task of having to acquire and install the code. The alternative is a Unix shell account that gives you most of what you need to start, and requires nothing beyond the communication program already on your computer. A shell is a menu-driven collection of application programs. Your computer's operating system probably displays one. Unix shells for the Internet typically list e-mail, newsgroups, telnet, file transfer protocol (FTP), gopher, and possibly a text-only version of World Wide Web (WWW), the Net's most abundant resource. A menu of applications is presented in standardized format, the selections made by simple key-driven commands that require little use of a complex command language. That list of applications is a lot to learn. You will need time to master a few basics of the Unix command language, going beyond the menu interfaces. Unix is like a moat standing between you on a quest, and the Internet castle full of informational jewels. The bridge across it is computer literacy. Stay tuned. I'll tell you in chapter 5 about things you can get from the Net that make it easy to use.

E-mail and PROFNET

E-mail grows in usefulness as you identify informative sources. One of the more interesting ones is PROFNET (Professors' Network). This is a distribution list of over 800 public information officers representing 380 colleges and universities, including some of the most prestigious; a wide range of federal entities such as the National Science Foundation (NSF), the Smithsonian, and the National Institutes of Health; AT&T's and IBM's corporate research labs; major medical centers; and the leading schools of business and public policy. It is worldwide in scope, stretching across Europe to Australia and China. Where else could you find such a profound collection of wisdom in one spot? PROFNET's purpose is to increase the immediacy and quality of communication between journalists and university and faculty members. To do this, it welcomes queries from news writers. There is no fee for conducting searches, nor is there a limit to the number of your queries. Thanks to the ability of computers to automate human activity, there is little work to processing your request. Queries are distributed within twenty-four hours of submission to PROFNET's membership. Individuals respond to queries in no formal manner. The queries are answered arbitrarily as interest is piqued.

PROFNET is available online through CompuServe and e-mail. It can also be accessed by fax and even by a 1-800 number. (See Appendix A for details.) The telephone approach requires more human intervention, thus cannot be expected to be as efficient. The extent and quality of responses depends on concise and incisive queries. Briefly specify your news organization (or what you have published), the nature of your project and the expertise you seek, when you need a response (the later the better), the channel and address for response (e-mail, CompuServe, etc.), then state your query in as much detail as possible.

Real People

Online sources have been criticized for being made up of virtual people hiding behind electronic façades. If you feel that way, look into joining a local writers' group. It's a good way to get an informal search started. The yellow pages of most major cities list writers' groups, or try your local bookstore. Membership fees are apt to be low, if any. Many have little more than a phone-answering facility and periodic newsletter, with meeting places chosen ad hoc. One special interest group I'm familiar with, a subset of a professional writers' organization, meets regularly in an upstairs room of a pub. Enough people attend the monthly after-hours meetings and remain for limited food and beverages that the tavern keeper is happy to accommodate. The conversation has been stimulating and the guidance sound, though I can't say much for the burgers and fries.

2

Resources at Your Side and Around the World

"Write about what you know." You've heard that before. Athletes discuss their sport, business people write on organizational and financial topics, cookbooks are written by chefs. Mystery writers aren't apt to be either criminals or detectives (although some have been), but they bring expertise to the keyboard. With or without experience, thorough research is fundamental to producing a written work worthy of casting into print.

Your know-how may start with general interest in a topic before curiosity takes you further. Eventually, the extent of your research determines your expertise. Don't fear setting out as an amateur. Give readers an ample supply of interesting facts and they enjoy even routine reports. Christopher Columbus, Meriwether Lewis, and the contemporary writer John McPhee, none an expert geographer, did that in their reports on the geography of the western hemisphere. (For an example of unskilled writing and outrageous spelling, but a riveting tale, read the journals of the Lewis and Clarke journey across the Rockies, written during three years of field research.)

Let's assume you have an assignment to write on something you know little about. You might begin with nearby sources—the telephone, your public library, local experts. Then, taking up leads, you work deeper into the subject. This chapter helps you understand and evaluate available resources. Descriptions of books mentioned are in the Bibliography, while you will find sources of information about computer services described in this chapter and in Appendix A.

At Your Side

A desk-side library is essential to any serious writer. Increased availability of electronic sources may reduce the number of volumes you keep on your shelves, yet there are some basic books every writer should have for ready reference such as the following:

- encyclopedia, the bigger the better
- dictionary
- atlas or gazetteer
- book of quotations, and a
- current world almanac.

A large encyclopedia should be the first reference consulted. A good single-volume encyclopedia can rapidly justify the active writer's investment. My fourth edition of *The New Columbia Encyclopedia*, containing 50,000 articles, is nearly twenty years old and still gets referenced regularly. I also use online encyclopedias. Although the ones I use are not as comprehensive as my old-faithful hardbound, the electronic versions are my only at-hand sources for very recent topics. The chief advantage of online sources lies in the newness of material. I keep lists of missing entries of *The New Columbia*, and those not found through online searches. Over two decades, The New Columbia has failed me exactly twenty-three times, with about half the missing entries reflecting topics newer than the book itself. My electronic list, maintained for about five years and based mostly on searching through the 33,000 online articles of Groiler's Academic American Encyclopedia, represents nearly as many failures, mostly on older topics. Online sources have not customarily contained as many entries as the printed volumes on which they are based, but this is changing. The *Encyclopaedia Britannica*, now publishing in three different forms of media—hardbound text, CD-ROM, and on the Internet—is a leading example of what can be done. The content of all three is equivalent, but the online version is not accessible without a password, and is regularly updated.

Online encyclopedias have another distinct advantage. It is handy to have access to physical pages that you can flip through and scan, but you can conduct a faster preliminary search using computer-based techniques—quickly printing out descriptions and listings, or extending a search with a quick shift to associated entries. Articles citing authorities along with cross-references and bibliographies get you started with key search words and phrases. Personal computer communications programs include a data capturing function—press the appropriate key and the incoming text displayed on the screen is saved in a disk file for reference after you hang up. By using the data capture capability, you can include that information in your notes without tedious transcription. From there you can continue your exploration for detailed data through library services (either physically on the premises, or also online) using the computer-delivered encyclopedia extracts.

CD-ROM References

A CD-ROM drive, too, gives access to encyclopedia information, more attractive in its presentation than online sources, although not usually as comprehensive. CD-ROM searches can be completed faster than those across telephone lines. If the files include hypertext (highlighted words or phrases shifting you to cross-references at the click of a cursor) which most do, that simplifies a long search process. The Grolier Multimedia Encyclopedia, with 5,000 entries based upon the twenty-one-volume *Academic American Encyclopedia*, and Microsoft's Encarta Multimedia Encyclopedia 98, based on a twenty-nine-volume publication (over 32,000 entries), are quite suitable for many purposes. They can even be appended on a monthly basis through a privileged connection online. You can enjoy incorporated sound and color graphics. The *Encyclopaedia Britannica* claims to have included every entry in its thirty-two volumes of printed articles in its *Britannica-98* CD-ROM version, with the inclusion of graphics, hypertext, and computer-assisted searching capability. Using its two disks can be cumbersome on single-drive systems. Whereas purchase of this impressive package might be out of the range of an individual's budget, it is finding its way into well-equipped businesses and libraries.

Electronic versions of several references have fewer entries than their printed counterparts, but they have added hypertext, color, and sound. The one-disk Random House Unabridged Electronic Dictionary is handy to keep "permanently" installed on a single drive if you rarely use any other

CD-ROM disks. Students and their teachers are the typical target audience for many popular CD-ROM products. If you write for a similar market, the limited breadth of these references, suitable for youthful readers, could act as a filter. A "sampler" CD-ROM reference is the Microsoft Bookshelf, which includes an impressive set of tomes: 15,000 entries in the Concise Columbia Encyclopedia, 100 maps in the Hammond Intermediate World Atlas, and short versions of *The American Heritage Dictionary, Roget's Thesaurus*, the *Concise Columbia Dictionary of Quotations*, and the *World Almanac and Book of Facts*. Perhaps the most economical and all-encompassing collection of abridged references is the CD-ROM Oxford English Reference Library. Selling for under $100, it contains the Oxford editions of the *Concise Dictionary of Current English, Thesaurus, Dictionary of Quotations, Dictionary of Modern Quotations, Dictionary for Writers and Editors, Guide to English Usage,* and *Dictionary of New Words*. In addition, it has the *Complete Works of Shakespeare, The Revised English Bible*, and, curiously, Lewis Carroll's *Alice's Adventures in Wonderland*. Even considering the one-time cost of a CD-ROM reader, the cost of a CD-ROM library is likely to be less than the collection of printed sources from which they are derived.

First generation CD-ROMs (most of those mentioned above) were, quite frankly, experimental. Computer reference books are finding their metier. The newer ones such as Encarta 98 and the Encarta Online Library offer free monthly online updates via dedicated Internet sites, much like the yearbooks published for printed encyclopedias. That is what could set them apart from printed volumes.

Of the five printed reference volumes listed earlier that every writer should have, only the almanac needs annual replacement. Changing world politics tend to limit the life of atlases, but you can generally nurse one along for several years if you cross-check your almanac to verify information about unstable geographic areas. Atlases are also available in CD-ROM versions, often including historical facts and street maps of large cities. Check out Global Explorer with its 20,000 entries and street maps of 100 cities. Imagine what an adventure writer describing a car chase through Paris or New York could do with that! For relief maps of continents and ocean floors, Mountain High Maps offers thirty-nine global views and seventy-four detailed relief maps with major cities and towns marked. Or, blast off through and beyond the solar system with RedShift 2 taking you astronomically through light-years of time and space.

Many professional organizations publish their directories, catalogs, journals, and technical manuals on CD-ROMs. The content is of interest primarily to organization members or subscribers and is often dated and subject to periodic revision. Some libraries stock bibliographic CD-ROMs for searches beyond their local holdings. The Gale Directory of Databases (CD-ROM or diskette), published annually, describes hundreds of these highly specialized sources, and would be useful to those planning to undertake deep searches in narrow fields. As I mention in chapter 5, the government is a major source of statistical data. The book *Government CD-ROMs* is a useful guide to what has been captured on disk.

Library Resources

Writers wishing to limit their investment in desk-side and CD-ROM libraries may find an adequate alternative in online sources available through school and public libraries. Increasingly, libraries offer simple data phone connections to such sources. Chapter 4 tells you how to explore these databases. This approach costs little and should be suitable for limited research needs. Still, there is something comforting about browsing through your own bookshelf, and I encourage you to start stocking it at whatever pace your circumstances allow. Literary people usually find that well-used reference books become good friends.

In addition to the basics you might want to include the following books as you build a reference library:

> *Webster's Biographical Dictionary*
> *Dictionary of American Biography*
> *Who's Who in America*, and
> *The Chicago Manual of Style.*

These books can become worthwhile in your research. Later in this chapter I'll tell you about other documents to add to your collection that are useful for special needs.

Look in your library's reference section for the annually published *Information Industry Directory.* This is a two-volume compilation of online databases, CD-ROMs, electronic information producers, brokers, and providers. A virtual who's who in the electronic media, it lists over 5,300 organizations, with an awesome inventory of topics and service classifications. Some are of quite a special category, delving deeply into very narrow topics. This can give you a great jumpstart into electronic availability on all sorts of topics.

Online Sources

Commercial services make many online databases available to the public, each with their own collections and specialized forums or bulletin boards. A subscription to only one such service is usually sufficient. Basic subscription charges continue month-to-month, to which connect-time charges and surcharges may be added for access to some facilities. Some services also offer a one-year subscription plan with unlimited access—choose the one that fits your needs. Minimum monthly usage, in the order of five hours, is inexpensive. One or two fortunate discoveries contributing to a writing project may well justify a year's expense.

Commercial Online Database Servers

These are the well-known online facilities, with access to many useful databases. Enrollment details are given in Appendix A.

America Online (AOL)—Personal services aimed at the family. Hotly competitive and growing rapidly, AOL ranks highest in popularity, with ten million subscribers. A software interface (navigator) to Internet is provided for each of the three major operating systems. They differ in quality. Mac users may prefer an alternative navigator such as Netscape. Full Internet service is available only through an AOL gateway. The company has been in no apparent hurry to move its services directly on to Internet's World Wide Web. Users may have some difficulty with browsing due to the sheer number of subscribers getting online at any given moment, until AOL delivers a browser replacement.

AT&T WorldNet Service (AT&T)—The newest national provider on the scene, AT&T WorldNet Service is primarily a communications vendor and only indirectly a database server through connections to the established commercial services. The company muddied the online waters when it announced WorldNet (available to anyone, but at lower rates for AT&T subscribers) and promised connections to AOL, CompuServe, and Prodigy, as well as to the Internet. With the largest customer base of all, its presence in the arena can only benefit consumers by holding prices down. WorldNet includes Eudora Lite and Netscape for Internet connection, with its own "front end" for logging on to a generally nearby AT&T facility. It is currently for Windows users, with plans announced for support of the Macintosh.

CompuServe Information Services (CSi)—longest established, with the second largest subscriber list and possibly due to join AOL, it offers individuals and businesses a broad variety of services: over 600 forums for discussion, a private message exchange for CompuServe members, and an Internet e-mail gateway. Probably has the best collection of research and, except for Dow Jones, business resources of the major providers. Extra fees apply to many resources. You can access CompuServe from any communications program, but direct interaction with CompuServe can be arcane. Better to use one of several navigators, available either from CompuServe or third-party vendors.

Dow Jones News and Information Service—Business data at a high price. Offers optional MCI Mail (to MCI subscribers only) in lieu of e-mail service. Essential for many business writers, but not suitable for general purposes.

Microsoft Network (MSN)—New in the summer of 1995, MSN requires Windows 95 for access, and has Bill Gates behind it.

Prodigy—The first online service with commercials, colorful ads on every screen make it sort of an online version of *USA Today*, and a model for World Wide Web advertising techniques. Originally a family-oriented service, Prodigy is changing to a business-oriented approach to full Internet service. Like AOL, Prodigy provides subscribers with the required software interface. Basic charges run higher than AOL (Internet access is extra); families get unlimited use, with multiple user IDs. A Prodigy-tailored version of the popular Netscape navigator (see chapter 5) is available.

These suppliers usually maintain local phone connections in major cities, eliminating costly long-distance connections for most users. That can be an important qualification for travelers who may need access to information anywhere, at any time. Beyond these well-known information sources, there are also many local suppliers. In every state you can find several low cost or free online sources through bulletin board systems (BBSs) accessed via personal computer communications programs. Modem USA describes these along with addresses and phone numbers to call for further information. While amateurs operate many BBSs, they tend to specialize in fields drawing professional interests. Quality of performance depends on the BBS operator, while content quality is a function of the contributors.

A Nationwide Bookshelf

Online public access catalogs (OPACs) are computer-based replacements for traditional library card catalogs, those long file drawers of dog-eared three-by-fives. OPAC is a generic name, that term often replaced with a proprietary title, like BOBCAT (NYU libraries). These systems allow terminal access to lists of the libraries' holdings, with the associated benefits of interactive computerized searching, bibliographic organization, printed listings, etc. Some libraries limit terminal use to their own premises (sometimes called hard-wired terminals). Most enable remote access from terminal emulators across regular telephone lines. The library can nearly always be accessed through these modern facilities, on holidays, in bad weather, and at four o'clock in the morning. If you don't have OPAC support in your community, discuss it with a local librarian. You may find that it will be available soon as the nation moves onto the information highway.

Libraries, public and private, in major metropolitan areas sometimes join in consortiums, sharing access to their individual catalogs, possibly even to their shelves. Increasingly, users can extend their catalog searches beyond the local consortium to other libraries around the nation, including the Library of Congress, via Internet connections. Anyone with Internet access can get to most OPAC facilities.

For special needs you can narrow your search to sources fitting your interests through two useful books held by many libraries. The *American Library Association Directory* lists most libraries in the nation, the size of their collections, and descriptions of special holdings. It is indexed geographically. Refer to *Subject Collections*, which lists special collections by subject matter.

For serious nationwide library searching, the prime source is the *OPAC Directory*, a listing of nearly all library online public access catalogs in the United States and Canada, with some Australian ones included. The reference section of most public libraries is apt to have this large, useful paperback. Each library is described on its own page, listing its address, contact people, basic collection size and types, dial-in phone numbers, terminal parameters and supported baud (data transmission) rates. *The Internet Directory* also lists OPACs, and identifies the "telnet" method of accessing them. I'll explain the use of telnet in chapter 5.

Both the *OPAC Directory* and *The Internet Directory* specify the catalog search system employed by each library. More than thirty-five systems are in use among a thousand libraries, conforming to at least twenty-three distinctly different standards, some merely minor modifications of others. Major OPAC systems include CARL, CLSI, Dynix, Hollis, MELVYL, and NOTIS. Whether dialing directly, or connecting via the Internet, it is important to know what system(s) you'll encounter when you get started. Without familiarity you could spend an undesirable amount of time reading Help screens or just trying to figure out what commands work without causing abrupt disconnection. That can be a discouraging experience when just a little know-how could open the doors to a treasure house. After you are familiar with one system, a companion volume to the *OPAC Directory* helps the others fall into place. Chapter 4 explains how to master this Babel of command languages, after walking you through an example of a flexible and friendly OPAC system.

UnCover is an online source of bibliographic information on both popular magazine articles and those published in specialized scholarly journals. This facility keeps a database of articles in over 8,000 periodicals, going back some twenty years. You can get a listing of the journals in the UnCover database, article titles and brief summaries of each issue. Searches by author can also be done. The full text of many articles can be delivered online, or by fax for a nominal charge. The information can be at your fingertips within minutes, without stirring from your workplace. Chapter 4 shows you how.

Timeliness—New and Old

Material listed in catalogs is no more current than the latest acquisitions made by the libraries themselves. Even then, there is a time lag between catalog entry and delivery. It is important to check *Books in Print*, a multivolume directory published annually, listing current American books by author and subject. Six times per year the publisher also issues *Forthcoming Books* as a supplement to *Books in Print*'s Subject Guide. There are CD-ROM and CompuServe online versions of *Books in Print* that include *Forthcoming Books*. For a small fee over customary CompuServe connection charges, you get computer searching through a database similar to the printed book. The CD-ROM version is dated, and marketed to libraries and bookstores by subscription. Although the combined volumes of *Books in Print* and *Forthcoming Books* do not include all that is available in print, they are apt to list every current book bearing an ISBN number (explained in chapter 3). These volumes are the best current source of information about available publications. Internet users should also check out Amazon.com Books, described in chapter 5, *Reference Sites*.

Books in Print does for books what *Readers' Guide to Periodical Literature* does for serial publications and *Facts on File* for weekly world news. It is always wise to refer to sources such as these, whatever the topic. Someone with interests similar to yours may have published one or more articles. If you plan to submit your work for publication, you must be prepared to analyze the competition. An hour spent with the *Readers' Guide, Facts on File*, and *Books in Print* will help accomplish most of that. CD-ROM versions of *Readers' Guide, Magazine Index* and *InfoTrac*, a monthly magazine index accessible in many libraries, can hasten your search.

What if your research requirement is for material published before that listed in current publications? Some topics concern material written years ago, requiring that you draw upon publications printed prior to a specific date. It is not always easy to find early texts on subjects of continuing interest or rapid change. You should note the publication date on all bibliographic entries. Literary critics love nothing better than to spot anachronisms in works they review. Specialized libraries, devoted to specific interests (law, health, ethnic history, etc.) are your best source for older material.

Another way to go is to review microfilms of old newspapers. They are helpful in gathering information contemporary to any event. Many libraries with microfilm or microfiche collections are apt to preserve major and local newspapers for a century or more. University Microfilms Inc. is a major supplier of a wide variety of past periodicals. The *New York Times Index* and its corresponding microfilm files are recognized historical sources, widely distributed to libraries. Each volume of the *Index* makes up an organized and cross-referenced history of every newsworthy event reported by The *Times*, usually covering half a year. You'll find it is easy to get side-tracked in an information search, as you peruse the many fascinating headlines from the past. Start with the *Index*, in which headlines give an overview of events. Then, if available, move on to the microfilm for detail. Review other parts of the papers for a tenor of the times—weather reports, sports news, fashions, advertising, even classifieds are captured.

One of the most delightful how-to books I have in my collection is an old paperback, *How to Lie About Your Age* by Sona Holman and Lillian Friedman. Instead of compiling a dull chronology of trivia, these two imaginative authors suggested that readers could deceive others about their true age by casually mentioning well-known events supposedly associated with carefully chosen circumstances in their own lives—graduation from high school, perhaps, in the month before Neil Armstrong walked on the moon (1969), instead of the time the Edsel was withdrawn from the market, ten years earlier. The book lists popular songs, fads, sports events, even common slang, year-by-year from 1910 to 1969. I use it as a reference, although there are several more serious books providing useful chronologies. *The Twentieth Century—An Almanac* does on a more scholarly level what *How to Lie About Your Age* does in a humorous vein. *Timetables of American History* puts more than two centuries of American history into perspective. *The Barnhart Dictionary of New English* gives you the origin of words, clichés, and other phrases introduced into the vernacular. Use it to avoid anachronisms in speech however. There were conscientious insiders, for instance, but no "whistle-blowers" at the time of the Teapot Dome scandal or in the graft-plagued days of "Boss" Tweed.

For very old tomes, don't hesitate to ask your librarian about rare book collections in the area. Libraries may hold these for limited use by serious scholars. While I was at the Boston Public Library working on a story about the development of celestial navigation, I had the pleasure of turning the pages of a book dating back to the seventeenth century, an

English translation of Antonio Pigafetta's diary of Magellan's first voyage around the world. Ordinarily, just to touch such books you would generally need to display some degree of authority and good cause. Expect security to be tight, precautions to be many—cotton gloves, no cameras or pens, guarded cubicles, etc.

Second-hand book stores are often a good source of the proper past. Finding exactly what you want may be daunting, but the payoff can be financially beneficial. Many find browsing among dusty books to be a very pleasant pastime. Most bibliophiles develop a relationship with one or more respected used book dealers. From what I have seen, few of these dealers lean heavily on the use of computers (although that may be changing), but I'll bet they can recognize what's of interest to their known clientele. Try bookstores near the sites of where your stories take place. You can find a treasure of local historical information, not necessarily found in larger libraries. That is what Paul Block, author of the novel *Song of the Mohicans*, did in Cooperstown, New York, where he found seventeen history books on the French and Indian War over 100 years old, written by the eminent nineteenth-century historian of that period, Francis Parkman. Some online booksellers, like amazon.com, will search for out-of-print materials.

Other great references may include the libraries of friends and acquaintances. It was a situation like this that worked for me. It was purely by chance that I came across three fifty-year-old technical texts while casually browsing through a friend's library. They were pertinent to a topic I was then investigating, and published only a year or so before events I was researching. Extracts from those books, coupled with photocopies of contemporary newspapers, gave me the title for a recent book and several nostalgic elements to be included in it.

Experts

The contribution of expert information, either fact or learned opinion, often makes the difference between stale and exciting writing. It is usually more interesting to read about other people and their views than about things; events become fascinating when seasoned with something new, added insights, or a different perspective. That's where experts or eyewitnesses might enter into your research.

Encyclopedia articles sometimes include an author's byline, possibly an appropriate pointer to an available expert. If the article is of recent origin, and your questions concern matters beyond the limited content of the entry, the author might be quite flattered to explain further. You can usually contact authors by writing their publisher, and asking that your letter be forwarded.

A book prepared for journalists to be added to your deskside library is the annually published *Yearbook of Experts, Authorities and Spokespersons*. Its purpose is to provide working members of the media with lists of interview sources. It is available to such people without charge, and an abridged version is also available on computer disk. The printed publication contains over 14,000 topics grouped by general subject matter. Participants are arranged alphabetically by name and by zip code. These are people who want to be interviewed, some perhaps for a fee, but most because they seek the publicity, or because they are industrial or government employees and that's their job. In effect you have a set of "yellow pages" describing experts with addresses and phone numbers of commentators, ranging from the White House and other branches of government to universities, companies, and individual consultants. Not long ago I was quite frustrated in my attempts to identify the alcoholic content of many domestic and imported beers. Individual breweries were of no help. Even the Bureau of Alcohol, Tobacco and Firearms seemed bent on obstruction—I would have had to make several individual requests, because no universal list appeared to be available. Then, through one call to a trade organization listed in *Yearbook of Experts*, and a second to the reference I was given, within an hour I had emerging from my fax machine the three pages of data I sought.

Other listings of highly specialized expertise may be more available than you think. Just about every special interest group has their own association. Look to your library's reference section for a shelf of directories. Among them you will probably find the annually published *National Trade and Professional Associations of the United States*. This is one of many directories, like that on experts, listing descriptions and means of contacting persons in the trade and professional associations for a variety of interests.

Museums and Archives

Museums, their libraries, curators and archivists are splendid sources of information, ancient through modern. *The Official Museum Directory* of the American Association of Museums describes nearly every museum in the nation, including their collections, addresses, hours of operation, phone numbers, and names of curators and board members. It is organized geographically, including a listing by zip code. A cross-reference of institutions by category directs you to special interests. The book should be available in most libraries. Review this before traveling for any reason. A freelance or travel writer might turn a vacation trip into an income-producing venture merely by spending a day or two in places found in the *Museum Directory*.

Getting photographs from commercial sources for reproduction can be costly. You will probably let your research and subsequent writing help you identify what prints to submit for publication. Appendix A lists several commercial sources, with the best known supplier of photographs and prints being the Bettmann Archive in New York, now called Corbis Bettmann and owned by Microsoft's Bill Gates. It holds 17 million images for private use and licensed reproduction.

The Federal Government

The federal government is a repository of an immense amount of information, all of which is our property as taxpayers. The problem is getting to it. Government publications, many of them internal to the government, are organized by originating agency. Thus you can find yourself in that "Catch-22" situation of having to know what to ask for when you pose your questions. A book that shows how to overcome this fix is *Tapping the Government Grapevine*. This inexpensive paperback is worth owning if you expect to spend much time digging out government data. It is also helpful in learning the terminology and organization of the federal government.

The Federal Information Center is a little known and easy-to-use source of government information, a department of the General Services Administration. Started in 1965, it gets little publicity, yet it is available to anyone through a simple, toll-free call (See Appendix A). If the respondents can't pull the information out of their databases when you call, they will take your phone number, assign a research identification number, and usually get back to you the next day. Sometimes you may have to call them again, but the research ID shortens the process. It may take patience on your part, depending on the nature of your questions (yes, you can ask multiple questions on the same call), but the Federal Information Center generally can help you cut through the complex strands of bureaucracy. Worst case is that the person responsible for helping you will give you another phone number, one that is a toll call. Sometimes they can give you the name of a specialist on the subject matter you're calling about. You may encounter multiple referrals, but by starting with the government's information database, you should reduce the number of bounces you'll take.

In querying the federal government, once I get past the front office people and hook up directly with the knowledge-workers, I often get more than I can handle in the way of information. I often feel as if my query has enlivened their bureaucratic day. Over a brief period I have asked about maritime statistics, harvests, formation of labor unions, World War II veterans, and a rare disorder of the eye. Three of the answers were given so quickly that I was almost embarrassed to have asked; one took three days and two phone calls to get the answer; the last one seems to have stopped everybody, but not without a lot of helpful searching. It would have taken me days to reach what may be a dry well anyway. You'll learn about a technique to make efficient use of this facility in chapter 6.

Researchers visiting Washington, D.C., and the Library of Congress (LC) are indeed fortunate. The Library of Congress is among the world's largest depositories, although the oft-spoken tale that it contains every American book ever copyrighted is not true. Whereas only members of Congress and affiliated federal agencies may borrow Library of Congress books, any visitor may examine the holdings on premises. Except for its 80,000 reference items, the holdings are kept in closed stacks. Initially you are introduced to the library's guide to its eight basic research services and told how to use the online command language. Internet users get guidance and access for browsing its catalog via a telnet connection. Due to the enormous volume of online users, off-peak hours (at night, after 8:00 p.m.) are the best time to connect.

People intent on government research should include the National Archives in their itinerary. Headquartered in the District of Columbia, it has regional branches throughout the nation (see list in Appendix A). A new facility at College Park, Maryland, houses federal government cartographic and architectural holdings, photographs, motion pictures, sound, and video recordings. Most of the remaining documentary material is in the headquarters building in downtown Washington, while a warehouse is also maintained in nearby Suitland, Maryland. Before visiting the Archives for any specific search, review the *Guide to Federal Records in the National Archives*. Although the three volumes of this directory only scratch the surface of what is available, they provide a detailed historical description and identify the location of pertinent material. A companion text, the *Guide to Holdings in the Still Picture Branch*, describes the extensive image collection. (See the next section of this chapter, and Appendix A, Publications— Regional Archives.) You can make a preliminary "visit" to these and many other museums via the Internet, perhaps gathering enough information to determine whether an actual trip would be useful to you.

The equally well-regarded Smithsonian Institution has taken a bold step forward with its online Smithsonian Institution Research Information System (SIRIS). Details of this introduction to the diverse collections of "the nation's attic" are discussed in chapters 4 and 5.

The Federal Depository Library Program

More than 1,370 libraries across the United States provide a direct link with the federal government through the Federal Depository Library Program. There you can review the *Guide to Federal Records in the National Archives*, the *Statistical Abstract of the United States*, the *United States Government Manual*, *Public Papers of the Presidents*, the *Survey of Current Business*, and the *Monthly Labor Review*. Your local library should be familiar with the nearest source of government information.

A Network of Friends

In your search for experts or witnesses, you should try to take advantage of what I call the "Small World Syndrome." (Others have called it "Six Degrees of Separation.") Its primary symptom is the repeated expression of the phrase "Would you happen to know anyone who . . ." It has been said that if you could put on an envelope a list of ten properly descriptive phrases about a remote friend (things like occupation, location of birth, employer, city or county of residence, memberships, unique experiences, etc.) concluding with the person's name, but excluding his or her address, then hand the envelope at random to any person who would pass it on to whomever they know best to continue the process, and so to the next, the envelope will be delivered to your friend in something less than ten transfers. I've never tried that specifically, but I believe it might work. How often have you found yourself among strangers at a convention or on a plane, exchanged a few words of trivial chatter about your circumstances, lapsed into the Small World Syndrome, and been surprised to find that this total stranger "went to school with . . ." or "once worked with . . ." or something to that effect? The human grapevine ignores its many dead branches and works in a seemingly dedicated direction with astounding speed. Statisticians can give you a rational explanation of this.

Start by discussing your information needs in every community of people with whom you share common interests. Once I wanted to find survivors of a naval event that took place over forty years earlier. There were no more than 200 people who took a direct part in that affair, men who probably came from and returned to nearly every state in the union. I had about twenty names. Many were already deceased. I was unable to find where any, living or dead, were last known to have resided, and privacy legislation prevents the government from giving out such information in most circumstances. At the time of the incident, the ages of the participants ranged from twenty to over fifty. The survivors were all senior citizens when I set out to find just one or two who were eyewitnesses to the event.

My search looked hopeless. Being no military person, I hardly knew the proper terminology, but I live in a community which is home to several retired military officers. I chatted with one man whom I knew only because we attended the same church. We had nothing but that in common. However, knowing his military background I told him of my interest (Small World exercise, transfer 1). As a Naval Academy graduate he was interested in my story, and a few weeks later, while on the opposite coast, he told a classmate about my pursuit (transfer 2). That person, 2,000 miles away and totally unaware of me, said he had a neighbor whose father, then deceased, had been the central figure in the very incident I was studying. He promised to contact the man and tell him third-hand of my activity (transfer 3). Within a month I was in a prolonged conversation with the son and arranged to get copies of his father's personal papers and detailed notes about the incident! That was a better find than anything I expected to get from living witnesses. Briefly I attributed my success to prayer—after all, it had started as I was leaving church—but more than likely it was the logical outcome of the statistics behind the Small World Syndrome.

3

Searching Strategies

Are you drafting a one-time periodical article? About to produce a scholarly and well-annotated history? Thinking about starting a thousand-page novel? Whatever your writing goal, you'll need a detailed plan for your information search to keep your time in tight control and costs down. In this chapter, I outline several tasks to help you prepare for your specific research activities.

The Library, Your Second Office

Allocate a day or more to becoming familiar with the facilities of your nearest library. Introduce yourself to a librarian and find out the lightest periods of the week in which you might get extra help should you need it. Explain that you plan to spend a good deal of time in the facility, describe your project, and ask if there are any specialists in your field of interest.

Large public libraries and museums conduct regularly

scheduled tours. During a public tour it may be difficult to take written notes, and would be discourteous to record voice notes while a tour director is lecturing. Check to see if a brochure is available. I keep a folder of brochures from every library and museum I visit. It has become a valuable source in preparing me for subsequent visits and follow-up phone calls. If there is nothing available, work out a map of the facilities, or a directory of departments, paying special attention to those areas of particular interest to you. When the tour is over, retrace your steps on a more leisurely basis to examine the collection more closely, adding to your earlier notes.

Browse the serial shelves to observe what periodicals the library maintains in your field of interest. Several may catch your eye. Government publications that are updated or replaced periodically may be in a separate area. Note how far back in the calendar printed editions are retained. Look for indexes of major publications. Bound newspaper indexes, like *The New York Times Index* and the *Wall Street Journal Index*, are apt to be found in the reference section, separate from microfilm cabinets or periodical shelves. Also be sure you know where the *Readers' Guide to Periodical Literature*, *Facts on File*, and *Books in Print* are kept.

Before ending your background visit, walk the stacks of the reference section, making sure you have sighted every collection and made notes on any volume or set of books that might have potential use. Reference is often a good place for freelance writers to generate fresh ideas. Look for the *Guide to Reference Books* or a similar publication that is a directory of directories. As you get familiar with these shelves the names of certain publishers such as R. R. Bowker, Gale Research, and Facts on File will become familiar. They are the principal producers of reference volumes, an indication of authenticity and currency.

Another great way to observe the workings of a library system is by volunteering. Most libraries have programs for volunteers. There are even nationwide organizations formed for library support. Investigate *Friends of Libraries USA*, a national association of branches affiliated with many community libraries. Perhaps partake in some training, and get to know the staff.

Going Online

Undertake the same learning approach with available online facilities—commercial operations like CompuServe, AOL, the Internet, and OPACs at your local library. If you are interested in the commercial databases, or for casual use of the Internet (arbitrarily less than twelve hours per month), sign up with one of the database services described in chapter 2. Remember that they offer access to their own collection of databases and forums, and provide connection to the Internet as an auxiliary, albeit popular, service. Otherwise, as an independent Internet user you will need to sign up with a service provider. That calls for shopping. Internet service providers in larger cities are apt to advertise in the business sections of daily newspapers, they are listed in many of the Internet textbooks and can be found in Internet newsgroups and Web sites (see Appendix A).

There are two categories of Internet service providers from which you would select your primary online service, depending on your needs: regional, and national or international, based upon the area codes they service. If you travel and will want local connection wherever you go you should choose a national/international provider, or one that offers an 800 number. (Your laptop with incorporated modem may not support graphical transmissions, but it should be perfectly capable of text-based interaction for e-mail and most textual Internet functions.) Local providers are apt to be priced a little lower, and if you work consistently in one location, that's the more economical the way to go. Among more than a dozen national providers competing for your attention, these are some of the well-known ones. They all provide some kind of technical support, often needed during set-up.

- *Advantis* (IBM)—local phone numbers in hundreds of IBM offices throughout the world. Intended for connection through the OS/2 Internet Access Kit; priced a little higher than average, for which you can count on excellent response and good service.
- *AlterDial*—UUNET Technologies. International in scope, hundreds of hubs (dial-in locations) in the U.S. Pricing is advantageous for high-volume mail and newsgroup use. Additional software and/or services required for other Internet functions; supports all desktop operating systems.
- *Microsoft Network* (MSN)—described in chapter 2.
- *PSInet*—Performance Systems International. Software for Windows and Macintosh interfaces; servers in six U.S. cities and London with a "backbone" that extends coverage to many additional area codes. Through policy and pricing they target their efforts to corporate and "power" users—over thirty hours per month.
- *WorldNet* (AT&T)—AT&T WorldNet Service, described in chapter 2.

After deciding what online service you will use, you'll need to learn to use it effectively. Learning takes time, perhaps six months to get thoroughly familiar with the programs.

Commercial services usually give a few hours of free connection time with an initial subscription, and also provide online tutorials and Help screens. During the free period, strive to become comfortable evaluating and using the system before doing any serious exploration. By developing your capability before billable time accrues, you will avoid floundering later when in the midst of a research project.

Ask your librarian for the voice-phone numbers of "free-net" connections. It is quite possible to get an Internet account for nothing (freenet). These are typically an adjunct service of a college or university, funded much like a campus radio station. Call those within your area code and inquire about their offerings, terms, and conditions. Some service providers operate under grants, but will solicit donations, much like public radio. For no-cost unlimited e-mail service (it's supported by advertising), call Juno for information and free software at 800-654-5866. Don't be too attracted by a potentially low cost. Typically, freenet nodes offer little more than e-mail and some local newsgroups (bulletin board postings). They may limit usage to a few hours per month or each connection to some fraction of an hour, and they support few telephone lines. They are useful in helping beginners become familiar with the basics of Internet usage and to gather information about other providers through one of the commonly available newsgroup postings.

Selecting a Provider

Large businesses and schools may have their own private Internet nodes, but many farm out the responsibility to commercial providers. Ask other Internet users what organization provides their service. Most regular users will be quite explicit about how they feel about their service. Listen for complaints like, "It's hard to get through during normal work hours . . ." "It takes forever to . . ." "My mail frequently gets lost . . ." "If you get help at all, it's from other users . . ." At the other extreme, you could hear "I'm on the Net several times per day, sometimes for an hour or more, and it only costs $20 a month." That is the company to call.

You might start with the lowest cost account you can find providing e-mail and newsgroups. Once you have any form of Internet account, it is easy to find another. As you get experience you can use the Net itself to identify other providers within your area code, and use e-mail to request information about their offerings. It is easier to change Internet service providers than to swap long-distance providers. The major difficulty is that you must inform your Internet friends of your address change. Even that can be done in minutes with a few keystrokes, if you plan for it.

Be wary about by-the-hour pricing. That's for the casual user (my line of differentiation is twelve hours per month on average). Plunging through all the pricing schedules is like hacking your way through a rain forest. A monthly rate for some fixed number of hours at any time of day or night for a given list of services tends to simplify matters. Your connection software should be able to display accumulated usage.

Once you have chosen a suitable Internet service provider, apply for an account. They will ask for basic information about yourself—name, address, and phone number, and selected method of payment. Unlike commercial organizations, Internet services usually allow you to specify your own user ID and an initial password (typically seven or eight characters). Generally you can choose from three types of accounts: e-mail only, Unix shell (functions offered may vary), and SLIP or PPP using TCP/IP. A SLIP account is needed for graphical transmission between your computer and others on the Net.

As you'll see, there are ways to reap the most useful benefits available to SLIP/PPP users with little added expense.

Most commercial online services (CompuServe, AOL, etc.) have bulletin boards or forums (similar to newsgroups) of interest to writers. Consider subscribing to one whether or not you use the Internet. The major organizations offer Internet connections as a corollary service, inexpensive for casual use. Since their interest is to get you to use their own databases, they will be quite explicit (and enticing) about what you will find. While you have to search for suitable databases on the Internet, commercial services often have online catalogs describing their offerings.

Getting Network Experience

Plan to spend the first month with your Internet or commercial account just getting familiar with the menus and commands before undertaking extended searches. Look into a few newsgroups. Browse the writers' or literary bulletin boards for information about writers' associations, newsletters, etc. Seek experience more than information until you are comfortable with the medium.

What's of Value?

The Net has so much to offer, and can be so complex, that keeping a simplified approach, all the while taking offline notes will reduce your level of frustration. Let the network grow on you, and don't be quick to jump into everything that catches your interest. You will soon discover the reality of what we mentioned earlier, the large amount of "noise" around far fewer "signals" of value. As you gain familiarity, you will collect lists of newsgroups that you'll want to browse regularly, perhaps on a daily basis, by subscribing to them. Chapter 5 tells you how to do this. There are three newsgroups that every user should have posted on the top of their subscription list:

> news.announce.important
> news.announce.newusers, and
> news.answers

They are the central sources of information concerning all other newsgroups. You can find the rare major changes to the newsgroup facility in news.announce.important. News. announce.newusers is quite stable, containing what you might expect, important information for beginners, explaining the general functions of newsgroups. The one that you should scan frequently, news.answers is long and dynamic. You will probably examine the content of only a handful of entries, but those should be quite informative.

General Search Strategy

At your desk, get ready for your research project by labeling a folder on your chosen topic. Keep notes on the central theme of your work, its purpose, the target audience, and how you intend to present the details (analyze, define, categorize, contrast, narrate, list, etc.).

Key Words—Signposts on the Search Paths

Draw up an outline with short marginal notes (key words) about the research you need to do. This is only a preliminary outline, and you can expect it to grow and change. In my experience of compiling research notes, I find it helpful to have different types of paper nearby, and to use different styles of written notation. I keep three types of notepads, all $8\frac{1}{2}$ x 11; lined white, lined yellow, and crosshatched white, and use different colored pens and pencils. I will then dedicate a particular pad and pen or pencil with a specific research mode. For example, I might carry only crosshatched paper on a visit to a museum where I expect to sketch something, transcribe numerical information, etc. If I anticipate taking notes at a lecture or in a one-on-one interview, I'll carry a yellow pad.

Pen type seems to vary with my mood, most often bold blue fiber, sometimes a thin ballpoint pen. Why all this variance? Perhaps it's my own quirks, but when I later want to find a particular set of notes that I've filed among hundreds of others, I am apt to recall that I wrote in green ink on yellow paper, or while at a certain location I was using crosshatched paper. Usually I can put my hand on what I'm looking for in minutes! Another thing you might want to do is write only on one side of the paper in order to spread out your sheets and see everything at once.

One important strategy to apply to your note-taking is to do something to isolate key words and phrases that you will use later for searching and filing techniques. Highlight these portions in printed upper case or by underlining—whatever suits you and sets off the words or phrases from the remainder of your notes. Reserve the top of each page for reentering them upon completion of your note-taking. This will help you first in conducting bibliographic searches, later in filing and retrieving, finally in indexing your work if that is to be part of your writing project.

One of your initial tasks will be to compile a bibliography. After that, you may want to produce a list of other sources to be checked: museums, parks, schools, geographic sites. The nature of your work may call for interviews or correspondence with witnesses (generically called "experts").

Think about the locale of your subject matter. Often this points to communities in which you would find the most information. If your local libraries are not adequate for your research, you will need help in selecting the library catalogs online in which to conduct subsequent searches. Don't leave home without having checked some online public access catalogs available to you. Your collection of key words will be of great help.

Informational Search Terms—
Your Travel Plans

First, compile an organized list of specific library materials you will want to examine or borrow. Do this by investigating the catalogs of local and remote libraries in a disciplined way. Put your interests on paper to save time on whatever inquiry systems you will use, with key words as search terms. Jot them down as they occur to you, in any order. You needn't be concerned about relative importance, but you may want to refine them for precision. For a specific search, the list of terms should be short, three to five being optimum, and not over ten. Historical searches might include a range of years; 1900–1930 would be considered one search term. Names, last and first if known, are the equivalent of one term. So too are descriptive words contained in book titles. There are at least four different lists that you should have.

Begin with thinking about the types of documents you might need. Catalogs include several different types: text, book series, video and film, sound tape and record, still photos, prints, etc. If you are looking for something other than a book include the type as a search word. (Could you complete worthwhile research on Irving Berlin without listening to some of his music?) The type of source could have some bearing on your project's financial plan—will it require equipment rental, shipping, travel, etc.?

List in a second group the names of authors, or those of any person or institution whose name is apt to be included in a book title concerning your topic. Names of people and organizations make up a special category of search elements.

A third group would contain the key words you would expect to find in book titles; the precise title isn't important, but word spelling is. Finally, if you are aware of the call numbers of books that interest you, generally recorded from prior searches, add those to your search notes. Use them when you want more details on availability of those or associated documents.

You now have four sets of search terms, grouped accordingly: key words, names, titles, and call numbers. The key words, often also part of the titles, will be the most useful elements in your search. Don't use long words if a few syllables could suffice. For example, the key word "America" would also bring out "American," "Americans," and "Americanization."

Use words specific to your interest which could narrow the search. "American history" is far too broad. "American history 1900–1930" might be better, but could you narrow it more? Perhaps "American labor history 1900–1930." Or state it as "American labor history after 1900." In a word search specification, certain terms are not treated as search elements but are used to frame your requirement; words like "and," "or," "not," "before," "after." Don't include articles like "the" and "a," as they are ignored.

When your four lists are complete, you should have perhaps a dozen search elements. This is what you will use in a detailed search. Normally, half the number will be adequate to find what you want. If your local library has online catalog searching, start there to build a bibliography. If not, use telnet (connecting by telephone lines to another computer) to connect via the Internet to a library that does. Print out what you have found so you have a hard copy listing of pertinent books in the collection. Later you can edit and organize what you have copied to produce an official bibliography. Scan the hard copy, highlighting the prompts and responses used in your first OPAC encounter. This will be instructive in preparing you for your next visit to the catalog.

Book Classification

You should be familiar with the two major methods for classifying books. The Dewey Decimal system (DD) is used widely in public libraries, the shorter numbers in its ten major groups making it suitable for smaller collections. Most research libraries make use of the Library of Congress classification system (LC) with twenty major groups. The two tables below can "get you into the stacks," either physically to where books in your field of study will be found, or to where you can browse further in online listings.

Table 3.1   Dewey Decimal Classifications

General	000
Philosophy	100
Religion	200
Social sciences	300
Language	400
Natural sciences	500
Technology, applied science	600

Fine arts	700
Literature	800
History and geography	900

Table 3.2 Library of Congress Classifications

General	A
Philosophy, religion	B
General history	C
Foreign history	D
American history	E, F
Geography, anthropology	G
Social sciences	H
Political science	J
Law	K
Education	L
Music	M
Fine arts	N
Literature, language	P
Natural sciences	Q
Medicine	R
Agriculture	S
Technology	T
Military science	U
Naval science	V
Bibliography and library science	Z

Another code for book identification is of more use to book publishers and sellers. This is the International Standard Book Number (ISBN), devised by R. R. Bowker and practically a requirement for stocking the book in retail stores. The ISBN is a unique number assigned by the publisher for identification and entry into Bowker's *Books in Print*. The first digit identifies the language and format, this associated with the publisher's identity by the next five digits. The next three digits designate the specific book in the publisher's collection, and the final digit is a mathematically computed check-digit to assure error-free recording. Few libraries use ISBN numbers. Thus the number is of little use in finding a book on the shelves, but it can be effective in controlling a bibliographic list, particularly if references are to be organized by publisher, format or language. You should always record it along with the library's customary call number.

Federal government documents have a different form of classification, using a code established by the Superintendent of Documents (SuDoc). This differs from Library of Congress coding, since the government organizes its publications not by subject, but by originating agency. Refer to *Tapping the Government Grapevine* for details on the agencies of the federal government and the SuDoc coding system.

A Bibliographic Library Visit

You probably can build a good bibliography online, but eventually you must visit the library. Browse the pertinent holdings, looking for bibliographies within each of the appropriate books. The newer the book, the more useful is what is in the back. Be sure to photocopy the bibliographic pages, as the content is likely to expand on what you have already collected. Label the photocopy with the call number, title, and publication date of the book it came from.

Next go to the reference section. Has your subject been covered before, and to what extent? This is important if your work is to be considered for publication. *Books in Print*, including the futures supplement, *Facts on File*, and *Readers' Guide to Periodical Literature* were mentioned in the last chapter. Investigate these (print, online, or CD-ROM) during the early stage of your research, again as you shift your efforts to writing, and finally as your written work nears completion. You are in effect keeping an eye on competition, while polishing up your own research.

Lining Up Experts

You can add originality and color to your writing by basing much of it on interviews with participants, witnesses, etc. What could be more authentic? They don't have to be celebrities. Recollections of people about what they were doing when they heard Kennedy was shot, or that Nixon resigned can still be interesting. What would a sports fan say about being at the ball park when Cal Ripken broke Lou Gehrig's long-standing record? Who might have put the most miles on a Volkswagen "beetle"? Chapter 6 provides you with specific interviewing techniques. Take the time to learn and practice them, so that you will be ready to put them to work when the opportunity arises.

Who Wants This Information?

Define your target audience in detail, and try to identify the things that would interest them, matching their characteristics to your sources: general public or scholars, specialists, technicians? Consider the ages, not only of your target audience but of those you may want to survey or interview. Young readers may not be interested in the recollections of senior citizens, but old-timers may find the same information fascinating.

Live Networking

Once you are into your topic and have a few items of interest to discuss, start telling people what you are doing. Capture their fancy and they will be your grapevine. Business cards bearing both your mailing and online addresses can be effective. One author had postcards made up with a picture of the cover of her recent book. Distributing those, she achieved a double-whammy, advertising her book and providing a useful "mail-me" card to get cooperation in further research on her next project.

Firsthand Knowledge

Write what you know. Remember that? To get experience check out the terrain, walk the streets, do the job, live the life that makes up your subject matter. It is important to do your homework on the topic, accumulating as much information as you can, before confronting experts. You can't expect specialists to teach you, and you don't want to waste their time. While exploring your customary sources of information, you probably developed questions about what you were finding. By experiencing your subject matter, you may resolve some as you pursue the subject further. The remaining questions are for the experts. Perhaps you can get answers to a question or two through a single phone call, or you may need time for a longer conference.

The expository writer John McPhee delves deeply into the lives of the people he writes about, young and old, male and female, teachers, mountain climbers, physicists, seamen, woodsmen, athletes and art connoisseurs. He brings an outsider's perspective to his essays as he becomes nearly as intimate with their activities as are his subjects themselves. They teach him, and he weaves his stories in such way as to fascinate the reader through the experiences of a seemingly effortless observer. It is almost as if he were writing to his mother.

Books Are Your Best Friends

You already know that. Researching will find you reading many books, studying many bibliographies, selectively identifying entries useful in your writing project. But it is important to maintain a reading habit that goes beyond your field. Read good books on any subject regularly. It may surprise you to discover helpful words, ideas, phrases, and leads you can use in your own work. An eclectic reading habit will keep you broadened, even as you intensify your work on a particular topic.

The Perimeter of Your Parameters

The notes you have gathered in this planning stage should suggest where you will have to go to get the information you need. Factor that into your financial plan. Can your travels do double duty? Perhaps business takes you to some places regularly, and all you need is an extra day or two there to visit resources pertinent to your writing. Much travel writing seems generated by vacationers and people who live near the locations they write about. Find to what extent you can collect information from distant locations by mail, e-mail, or telephone, perhaps even by hiring part-time agents. Once, I wanted the name of a short street in a New England town, too small to be on the maps available to me and too far away for me to investigate personally. A few inquiries through the CompuServe literary forum not only got me the street name but a description of the houses on each side. Many detailed street maps of cities and towns, large and small, are available on the Web.

Back to the Library

After you have gained familiarity with the Net, or perhaps because of it, you will still need to make frequent trips to your library. As any new assignment gets underway, head for the reference section and run your fingers through Volume 2 of the *Information Industry Directory*. This book is proof that you can find just about anything you want if you are willing to pay for it. Although it doesn't list the prices of information (those vary greatly), Volume 1, containing descriptive listings of producers and brokers of information, includes details on literally thousands of topics and phone numbers of information providers.

The extent of your funding and the importance of what you plan to produce affects how far you go in exploring these sources. Many require a subscription to the service and a detailed knowledge of the inquiry command language. If there is some urgency to your quest, try first to narrow the specifications of what you seek. Then identify the major sources of information, types of media, and names of major organizations that might have it. Next, talk to one of your reference librarians. They are apt to know where they can put their hands on these sources, if not within their own facility perhaps by phone to another library. Many libraries maintain a subscription to Dialog, a large collection of computer databases, allowing as-needed access. This is a costly and complex facility that is not apt to be publicly available and requires skill in its use. Even a very brief search can be expensive. Reference librarians might use it, perhaps to help in an unfamiliar research request, charging the cost of a few short searches to the library's account. That was my experience when I was working in an out-of-town library on a lengthy project. I heard that the local newspaper had recently printed an article pertinent to my interests but I had no idea when or on what page. The librarian did a Dialog search, and within a few minutes I found the article on an inside page of the paper published some ten days earlier.

Warming Up to the Task

Summarizing what I have covered, these are the warmup exercises you should take up before starting out on a full-fledged hunt for detailed information.

1. Become familiar with your local library's reference section.
2. Select the online sources you will use, sign up, and get familiar with the major information categories suitable to your needs.
3. Qualify your subject matter, and start on a bibliography, based on online searches and preliminary visits to the library.
4. Talk up your project to initiate the Small World Syndrome.
5. Get firsthand experience by talking to those with day-to-day activities in your field of study.

4
Base Level Searches

The hunt is on. It's time to use your word processor to assemble a *master list* of resources, drawing on your collection of key search elements. This will be broader in scope than the final bibliography. It is what drives your actual research although it is subject to frequent modification as you progress. You can extract most of its entries from online sources. That is not as seamless as it sounds as there are many software fences you must get over. In this chapter we'll walk you through that territory.

Master List and Bibliography

The master list is a single file made up of two parts. The first portion should include every source, planned or completed, to be reviewed—books, periodicals, journals, museum collections, telephone inquiries, online databases, names of people for interview. From it you will assemble the second part, the final bibliography for inclusion in the back matter of your completed manuscript. Give the file a descriptive name like MASTER.LST. It doesn't have to be very imaginative.

Entry Format

The master file starts as a planning document, but will develop into a control log of your research work. Organize it to suit your purpose: geographically by locations to be visited; in chronological order of investigation (always subject to change); perhaps in sub-sections conforming to your material outline. You will probably reorganize sections of it when you are deep into your project. Some items might be entered multiple times. Devote a line, paragraph, or page to each entry as needed. Include all reference information, added comments, and possibly a brief evaluation of its value to your efforts. Except for bibliographic references, paragraphs can be free-form in structure. References to printed material should be according to established style requirements. Some publishers have unique bibliographic specifications, while many conform to those set out in the most current edition of *The Chicago Manual of Style*. Taking the time to make a proper entry at first reduces the polishing effort later. For books, include the following:

- author's full name and title (Captain, Dr., etc.) if it is part of the book
- title and subtitle of the book, the edition if later than the first, number of the volume if it is one of a set
- city of publication, and state or country if the city is obscure
- publisher's name, and the
- year of publication.

For serial articles:

- author's name
- headline or title of the article, typically in quotes
- name of the periodical, volume and number within the volume
- date of issue, and the
- beginning and ending page numbers.

For news articles:

- author's byline
- headline or article title, in quotes
- name of publication, and the
- location and date of article (dateline)—often the incidents reported occurred on an earlier date, and possibly time zones and hemispheres have a bearing.

For Internet material:

- author's name and fully qualified Internet address
- document title
- source and protocol (described in more detail in chapter 5), such as "FTP" or "WWW-html"
- Internet address or Uniform Resource Locator (see chapter 5) where document can be found. Make a note of the URL (cut and paste it from the Web, if possible, to minimize mistakes) and the creation or latest modification date of article.

Note: Internet material is transitory; if it exists in an archive, also identify that.

If the publication is not one you own or have at hand, add to each standard bibliographic reference the name of the library (and branch, if pertinent) or the location of the document, its call number, and ISBN. For material that cannot be withdrawn from the library, be prepared to make photocopies of pertinent pages, entering a reference to these in your master list. Try to avoid hand transcription of even brief content; it is too easy to introduce errors. Identify photocopied material by assigning a unique cross-reference number, the simplest being the date on which you make the copy, jotting it on the photostat. In copying from microfilm, the output is not apt to contain the date and page number. Be sure to transcribe it onto the page while the projection is still in front of you. Photocopying for research purposes is permissible under the copyright laws. Libraries encourage the practice as a source of extra revenue.

Imagine that you must direct someone over the phone to find the article or book, and soon after that the sources may never again be available. Could your notes lead the person directly to the information? Record the details thoroughly the first time and save hours in subsequent searches.

Building a Bibliography Online

One software fence you will encounter is the difference in format between catalog entries and proper bibliographic references. The process goes like this.

1. At your own computer, initiate your search in a selected OPAC, using your list of search items. Successful searches present you with bibliographic descriptions in the format of the search system you are using.

2. Be sure the data capture function is turned on, and record the items you want in a capture file. Don't be concerned about collecting extraneous matter—you can edit it out later. Most data capture programs allow you to hold up the flow of data as you encounter unrelated displays. After a while you learn to avoid recording most interim prompts or to rake out remaining junk quickly.

3. When you have captured every suitable citation, end the connection.

4. Using an editing or word processing program, cull out the extraneous data in the captured file such as user prompts and system responses, leaving the citations as a bibliographic list. These will be in library format, and may be in upper case. Call numbers and other descriptive matter such as owners, locations, and types of material (recordings, juvenile texts, serials, etc.) found in the collection will be included.

5. Transfer the edited file into your master list. Macintosh, Windows, and OS/2 users may do this with clipboard or cut-and-paste functions. Or use the import function of a word processor. The result is an accurate but inadequately formatted set of new bibliographic references to add to your master list.

Perhaps instead you will use a library's local terminal to investigate OPAC resources. In this case using an attached printer will give you a hard copy of your search results to be transcribed manually into your master list. At this stage you will probably be accumulating other papers with bibliographic references. Every time you examine a book that appears to fit your purposes, photocopy its bibliography. Note entries there not found in your online search having publication dates and topics that match your needs. Electronic searching isn't perfect. You may need different search terms. It is possible that someone entered the original descriptive words imprecisely. With added information in a later attempt, the book of interest may be found in the online catalog, if not in the first library of choice, then elsewhere. In any event, you will probably accumulate several items to be added by hand to your research list.

While adding new entries to my master list I find it useful to put an identifying symbol (* or #) in front of each citation. It tells me that I have not yet examined the material. I remove or replace the symbol after I have seen the publication. I use both characters—the asterisk simply means "unexamined" and the pound sign indicates that I've seen it. I will then give it a number like #1, #2, or #3 to rank the usefulness of the citation as a reference. At that point I rearrange the entry into the desired bibliographic style. Two "dummy" entries sit at the top of my master file as style models. They look like this:

Lastname, First I., Title, *Book Title: Subtitle*, City, State (if the city is not recognizable on its own), Publisher, Year.

Byline—Last, First I., "Article Title," *Name of Periodical*, (Month Year), vol. nnn, no. n, p-p.

These are drawn from a publisher's style guide (*The Chicago Manual of Style*), showing me the proper format and punctuation for bibliographic citations as well as annotation formats used in footnotes or endnotes. Include models for each type of format as additional dummy references.

Bibliographic Quality

Eventually you will have collected a variety of references, many going beyond what you can extract from OPACs. As you review source material, be sure to identify it as either "primary" or "secondary." Primary sources include eyewitnesses, on-the-spot reporters, journalists as witnesses, and original documents (or authentic copies) written by those about whom you are writing. Historians strive to find primary source material. Journalists' comments may be based on actual meetings with the people they are writing about (their own primary sources). Those comments are secondary source material for anyone else, and should include attribution.

Others work from secondary sources. Essayists, fiction writers, and poets work from both sources. Their studies may make them subject matter experts with as great a command of the topic as the authors and witnesses with whom they are dealing. Their own analyses and summations, primary to them, are secondary and worthy of citation when used by others. You need only a word or two in your master list to qualify the reference. Remember that journalists are often working against very tight deadlines and covering developing events, and their accounts may be full of errors—note the number of corrections published every day in *The New York Times.*

Measure the quality of your final bibliography by five criteria. Is each reference item:

—Available? Can the material be found by most readers, or does it reside in but one location? Don't exclude hard-to-find books and useful unpublished manuscripts, but be aware that the presence of too many in a reference list can be frustrating to the interested reader. Be particularly wary of Internet sources, transitory in nature.

—Current? Is the publication up to date? Cite older volumes only if relevant. Check *Books in Print* (although it too can include not-yet-published and out-of-print titles if an update from the publisher is not obtained in time) and broaden your searches to identify the latest editions.

—Reliable? Does the publication give accurate representation of the subject matter? Is it written or edited by recognized authorities?

—Thorough? Are all major topics in your work adequately represented by an entry in the listing?

—Understandable? Is the text at the target audience's level of understanding? Is a glossary needed as an adjunct to your text or listed publications?

While your master list goes beyond your ultimate needs, it need not include sources that fall significantly short of these qualifications. The bibliography reflects a subset of the master list—only sources contributing to the written work.

Index Cards—Where Are They?

Perhaps you are wondering what happened to the classical set of bibliographic index cards, once essential to scholarly research. They still exist, but with computers they are used for different purposes. Sorting and block transfers within a

Author - last, first	*Keegan John*
Title and subtitle	*A History of Warfare*
City [state / country]	*New York*
Publisher, Year	*Harper & Row. 1993*
Library	
Call #	
	p. 38 - broadside cannons on HMS Mary Rose

FIGURE 4-1 *Index Card—Book*

word processor makes it easy to rearrange electronic listings. Printed versions of your master list can be easily reproduced and are more useful than index cards for making additional notations.

Some people like to write up selected references on cards for use when examining material that can't be borrowed or removed from its present location (reference manuals, artwork, etc.). The collections of large research libraries like New York Public Library and the reference sections of local public libraries cannot be borrowed. It helps to carry a handful of blank cards on every library visit. Include one prepared for use as a prompter for recording detailed information. (Figure 4-1.) Cards are handy for indexing large documents, tracking Internet discoveries, and recording the facts behind interviews.

Both card and computer references should be maintained for some items. Cards can be useful when extracting detailed data from magazines. (Figure 4-2.) Keep data on the back for sections or pages of interest, record of dates viewed, cross-

Byline - first last	*Jack Butler*
"Title"	*"An Introduction to Tape Backup"*
Periodical name	*Monitor*
(Month Year)	*(May 1994)*
Vol. nnn, No. nn	*Vol. 13. No. 5*
Pages - from, to	*18-20. 44*
Library	*CPCUG*
Call #	

FIGURE 4-2   *Index Card—Periodical*

references, etc. Leave the top line of the index card open for later notation of effective key search words. Pencil them in. They may change as you get deeper into your research. Keep notes of useful pages by number and range, accurate quotations, and other appropriate books found nearby.

Master List to Bibliography

As you review the contents of your master list, use your word processor to format the bibliographic reference lines into the lower, formal portion of the file, alphabetically by author. For some publications, it may be appropriate to break the bibliographic listing into topical sections, authors listed alphabetically within each section. This is properly called a "reading list," in which it would be permissible to include the same reference in multiple sections. Don't put anything into the formal bibliography that you haven't personally checked and evaluated for inclusion. Any book or article mentioned in footnotes or endnotes, referenced or quoted from directly, should be represented in the bibliography. After consulting each book, remove the unexamined-marker (asterisk) from the master list entry, and replace it with a numerical identification of its relative importance. You have, in effect, a dynamic log of your research work.

Online Searching

In 1994 Maryland became the first state in the nation to give its citizens Internet access to nearly every public library in the state, including all campuses of the University of Maryland, through the Sailor System. Californians throughout their state can connect to Stanford's libraries in Palo Alto, and through the Melvyl System to all University of California libraries. OPAC networks are widespread. Many of these systems are Unix-based, offering little to help the beginner struggle with the ruthless Unix command language. The early presumption was that computer scientists and physicists, the first users of these systems, were already familiar with Unix. As library access becomes available to the public, work is being done to put friendlier prompt-response screens between Unix and the user. The CARL system is a good example of this, and for that reason was chosen for the illustrations to follow.

CARL Corporation (once the Colorado Alliance of Research Libraries) operates the CARL Systems Network made up of over six hundred libraries across the nation. Its web site is at http://www.carl.org. Each affiliated library maintains a gateway on the Internet connecting to CARL's mainframe. This is transparent to users at the keyboards of terminals connected to their neighborhood OPAC facility. Anyone, anywhere, with Internet access, can telnet to CARL and examine the catalogs of its affiliated libraries (see Appendix A). They can also examine UnCover databases containing millions of articles available for delivery, using the same straight-forward command language. The UnCover Company (URL: http://www.carl.org/uncover/unchome.html) is associated with CARL. In the examples to follow I'll discuss OPAC systems generally, using CARL commands in the illustrations. Then I'll show you how to make the transition to the commands of other systems.

OPAC use is confined to searching and browsing bibliographic references. You can't open books via OPACs, or submit inquiries to reference librarians. Some libraries do allow card holders to reserve books through online sources. Some systems require passwords or they limit remote-user access to off-peak hours. Browsing remote catalogs is a good way to build a reference listing, compiling it from multiple sources. Should you find books needed in your research that are not immediately available from your library, you can probably arrange interlibrary loans through your local librarian.

Searches on computer are made through interaction with standardized menus. While you think in traditional terms such as author, title, subject, and call number, access to OPAC entries starts with one of the three generic headings: Word, Name, or Browse. W(ord), N(ame), B(rowse), and S(top), or S(witch) or similar commands are the only ones you'll need to know to start. Some systems allow you to enter just the initial letter, and usually bypass sub-menu presentations by entering search words as part of the command. Otherwise, you are guided through the various options in a series of menu screens. You don't need a detailed knowledge of bibliographic record structure, or an understanding of the computer techniques used in database searching.

The results of each search are reported on the screen in response to a request or D(isplay) command. Usually a search is conducted in stages, each stage narrowing or expanding the number of selections. If you work from a computer at home, dialing in to your local library's OPAC, keep the screen capture function running to record search results as they are delivered. D(isplay) brings up an enumerated listing of abbreviated bibliographic descriptions. You would then select individual item numbers, or perhaps a range, to see the full citation of items identified. This is what will be transferred from the capture file into your master list. Reduce capture file clutter by pausing the capture program during explanation of search options, and resume it just before issuing D(isplay).

An OPAC Search

Let's explore the process. For illustrative purposes I've chosen the topic of comedians for our subject, but I'll take some side trips to investigate other more serious literary and historical personages.

My search starts by dialing directly into the OPAC system supported by a local multibranch library. After establishing a connection, this version of the CARL system asked for identification of terminal type so that data could be sent in blocks fitting my display. I would see something similar in a telnet connection. A series of introductory screens precedes the presentation of the first OPAC screen; libraries often tailor the system to their own purposes.

Word Searching

I'll be looking only for books on movie comedians, so let's start with a Word search, using those key words. In Fig-

```
05/30/95
11:39 A.M.        SELECTED DATABASE:  Montgomery County

            The computer can find items by NAME or by WORD

            NAMES can be authors, editors, or names of
            persons or institutions written about in the book

            WORDS can be words from the title, or subjects,
            concepts, ideas, dates etc.

            You may also BROWSE by TITLE, CALL NUMBER, or SERIES.

            Enter    N   for   NAME search
                     W   for   WORD search
                     B   to    BROWSE by title, call number, or series
                     S   to    STOP or SWITCH to another database

            Type the letter for the search you want.
             and press <RETURN>,    or type  ?  for <HELP>

                 SELECTED DATABASE:  Montgomery County

  ENTER  COMMAND (?H FOR HELP) >> w_
```

FIGURE 4-3   *OPAC Search—Introductory Menu*

(Montgomery County Department of Public Libraries—MCDPL; using the CARL System
of Colorado Alliance of Research Libraries—CARL)

ure 4-3, note the paragraphs describing record fields to be examined. Choosing a single word would put me in too broad a category. Prior searches using just the word comedians brought out 144 items, so I'll include a qualifier. In practice, searches entail multiple efforts, expanding and refining each list delivered. These illustrations reflect that experience.

Figure 4-4 invokes the search with results shown on the next screen, Figure 4-5. Note what the wild card (*) did for me. (The wild card allows extensions causing the search to match comedian in all sorts of areas I wouldn't have thought of. Had I used just the singular word comedian I would have found nothing, since that word did not exist within the collection's "descriptors" (significant words that define documents). Use of movie, instead of the broader movie*, would have been effective since it is part of the subtitle of the first item, but I could not have known that in advance. The

```
           SELECTED DATABASE: Montgomery County


REMEMBER -- WORDS can be words from the title, or can be subjects,
concepts, ideas, dates, etc.

          for example --  GONE WITH THE WIND
                          SILVER MINING COLORADO
                          BEHAVIOR  MODIFICATION

Enter word or words (no more than one line, please)
separated by spaces and press <RETURN>.




>comedian* movie*
```

FIGURE 4-4   *OPAC Word Search* (MCDPL—CARL)

classifications of the two matching items, Library of Congress
M261G2 and H791R, might be helpful. M identifies Music,
presumably musical comedy, and H Social Sciences, more fit-

FIGURE 4-5   *OPAC Search Results* (MCDPL—CARL)

```
COMEDIAN* MOVIE* matched       2 items.
  1 Maltin leonard                              MONT           1978
     The great movie comedians : from charlie chaplin 791.43092 M261G2

  2 Hope bob 1903                               MONT           1977
     The road to hollywood : my 40-year love affair w 791.43 H791R

ALL ITEMS HAVE BEEN DISPLAYED.
Enter <Line number(s)> To Display Full Records (Number +  B  for Brief)
<P>revious For Previous Page OR <Q>uit For New Search 1
```

ting than one of the history selections. Note that this library also identifies its books under the Dewey Decimal system, 791.43 a classification under Fine Arts. Leonard Maltin's book looks interesting, so I select line number 1.

The full record has given me useful information for my master list. Figure 4-6 illustrates the elements searched in a MAchine Readable Catalog (MARC) entry. A Word search is usually a good way to start on an unfamiliar topic. It looks for matching words that appear in the title, series, content notes, and subject fields of bibliographic records. To seek an author whose last name is common and first name is unknown or uncertain, use the name in a Word rather than a Name search and increase the chances of a hit. The more elements you include in your search, separated by a space or slash, the more specific your search. It is not necessary to submit them all at once. Some systems limit the number of search elements in a single inquiry, or confine them to a single line. After being shown the results, a sub-menu lets you A(dd) more words to

FIGURE 4-6   *OPAC MARC Record* (MCDPL—CARL)

```
-------------------------------------------------Montgomery County----------
AUTHOR(s):      Maltin, Leonard.
TITLE(s):       The great movie comedians :  from Charlie Chaplin to Woody
                  Allen /  by Leonard Maltin.

                New York :  Crown Publishers, c1978.
                xvii, 238 p. :  ill. ;  26 cm.
                Includes filmographies and index.
Contents:       Charlie Chaplin -- Mabel Normand -- Fatty Arbuckle --
                  Buster Keaton -- Harold Lloyd -- Harry Langdon -- Charley
                  Chase -- Raymond Griffith - - Marie Dressler -- Laurel &
                  Hardy -- Will Rogers -- Joe E. Brown -- Marx Brothers -- W.
                  C. Fields -- Mae West -- Three Stooges -- Abbott & Costello
                  -- Bob Hope -- Danny Kaye -- Red Skelton -- Jerry Lewis --
                  Woody Allen.

OTHER ENTRIES:  Moving-picture actors and actresses  United States
                  Biography.
                Comedians  United States  Biography.
                Comedy films  Catalogs.
more follows -- press <RETURN> (Q to quit)
```

narrow the selection criteria. Experimenting with word combinations is easy, fast, and often revealing.

The catalog system organizes descriptors into several categories of search elements, and recognizes quick pathways into the listings. The sequence of words in an entry line is not important. If a search request contains a "monster word" (one so common that it has thousands of entries), and other words are entered, the system may switch the search order. For example, in a word search done on HISTORY CLOWN* in a large database, HISTORY is recognized as a monster word. Then the order is reversed and all occurrences of CLOWN, CLOWNING, and CLOWNS are gathered from the Words file, and HISTORY is run against the smaller list. You can see that this is more efficient than running CLOWN* against the thousands of HISTORY occurrences.

Logical Searching

Sometimes certain words and phrases may be used in a special way to narrow your search. They are the logical operators AND, OR, BUT NOT, and AND NOT, Boolean search elements to control the search technique. The extent of Boolean searching capability depends on the OPAC system. Full Boolean function is not available in all systems, but it works like this. If you enter a search for Hillary, you will get both Sir Edmund Hillary and Hillary Rodham Clinton. If you search for Hillary NOT Clinton, you will get Sir Edmund and perhaps others but not the First Lady.

Searching by Name(s)

Although my search for movie comedians gave me only two books, by expanding one entry to its full description (Figure 4-6) I gained a good list of comedians we might want to investigate. By selecting N on the menu (Figure 4-3) you can do a name search for authors, or names of persons or institutions written about in a book. Thus you could search for authors of books (Virginia Woolf or J. D. Salinger), or for books about people (Franklin D. Roosevelt), even companies (IBM). If your subject is composed of frequently used words (e.g., history of politics in twentieth century), and it is difficult to substitute different words, make a second search by name drawn from the first list. This should narrow the results to something more manageable.

If you are conducting a complete search for information written both *by* a person and *about* a person (e.g., John F. Kennedy), do separate searches first by name and then by Name/Word. A combined Name/Word search is ordered with the N command by entering the name first in the string, followed by the word or words; separate the two with a slash (/). This technique searches the full record in the Author category and names found in the Other Entries category. Word search looks into Title, part or all of the Contents, and subjects other than names in Other Entries. If you start with a Name search you probably could add a Word to reduce the size of the set. However, if you start with a Word search you will not be given the opportunity to add a Name. An example of a Name/Word command:

```
NJohn F. Kennedy/senator president
```

Doing that to see what's available on the Marx Brothers, we found several biographical works. Biographies are often entered with the years of birth and death as descriptors. (Name, birth, and death dates combine to make a single descriptor; enter a date incorrectly and nothing would be

found.) A span of years can be found in biographical dic-
tionaries, or sometimes in a Name/Word search, such as
`Nmarx/biography`.

Note that the display brought out authors and subject
names indiscriminately. After some experimental searching,
and making note of the 791 call number prefix, we settled on
line number 5. Now we have another book for our master
list, classified locally, and have identified 1891–1977 as the
years in which Groucho lived. We also can see where the
book is held and whether it is currently available.

Browsing

OPAC searching allows you to scan a collection, much as you
would if you walked through the library's stacks. The Browse
command causes a sequential search through sections of the
collection, while the Browse sub-menus let you search by title, name, subject, or call number. Title browse, sometimes

FIGURE 4-7   *OPAC Name Search Results* (MCDPL—CARL)

```
 1 Marx samuel 1902                                 MONT            1987
     Gaudy spree :  the literary life of hollywood  791.43 M3922G

 2 Marx maxine                                      MONT            1980
     Growing up with chico                          BM3878M

 3 Marx samuel 1902                                 MONT            1975
     Mayer and thalberg :   the make-believe saints 791.43023 M468M

 4 Marx groucho 1891                                MONT            1989
     Memoirs of a mangy lover                       B MARX

 5 Marx arthur 1921                                 MONT            1992
     My life with groucho                           B MARX 1992

 6 Marx  arthur 1921                                MONT            1993
     My life with groucho                           LARGE TYPE B MARX 1992

 7 Marx arthur 1921                                 MONT            1986
     Nine lives of mickey rooney                    B R777M

 <RETURN> To continue display
 Enter <Line number(s)> To Display Full Records (Number +  B  for Brief)
 <P>revious For Previous Page OR <Q>uit For New Search
```

```
                                                       -Montgomery County----------
AUTHOR(s):        Marx, Arthur, 1921-
TITLE(s):         My life with Groucho /  by Arthur Marx.
                  [Newly rev.]

                  Fort Lee, NJ :  Barricade Books ;  Emeryville, CA :
                     Publishers Group West [distributor],  c1992.

OTHER ENTRIES:    Marx, Groucho,  1891-1977.
                  Marx, Arthur,  1921-
                  Comedians  United States  Biography.

LOCN:     FAIR   ADULT      STATUS: In ---
CALL #: B MARX 1992

LOCN:     GBURG  ADULT      STATUS: In ---
CALL #: B MARX 1992

LOCN:     LFALLS ADULT      STATUS: In ---
CALL #: B MARX 1992

more follows -- press <RETURN> (Q to quit)
```

FIGURE 4-8   *OPAC Short Citation* (MCDPL—CARL)

expressed as a single command, TB, lets you view the collection in title order. A title search is usually quite specific. Enter the words exactly as you know them to exist, as when looking for an individual volume in a series. Punctuation should be included if it falls within the text of the title. If you do not know the exact title, a Word search is better. Databases have been indexed for name browsing (search command NB), a useful approach when you are aware that several publications have, or at least start with, the same name.

Subject browsing (command SB) allows you to view the collection in series order. You can look at listings of books, proceedings, and other reports published as a part of a series. If you don't know the specific words in a title or series, you can still search by using the key words that most accurately describe the work. You can do this with a variation of subject browsing or subject/word browsing (command SW).

Searching by Call Number

Have you ever had the experience of going into the stacks for a book and finding interesting volumes nearby that you were unaware of? Call number browsing allows you to conduct a catalog search according to the order that materials are arranged on a library's shelf. A call number consists of a classification number, Dewey Decimal, Library of Congress, or both, and other abbreviations relating to a title, author, or media type.

Knowing the general call number of a book of interest, you can use it to find associated materials in a collection. With a list of citations, you can go back into the database to search by the first portion of the call number. That gives you a shelf list that shows nearby books on the same or similar topics. The partial listing in Figure 4-9 could help us expand our study of movie comedians. Sometimes it helps to start with a call number a few digits lower than the selected one, allowing you to look to the left of it on the shelf, so to speak. Some systems let you search forward or backward in the list by using + and − commands. Even conservative library patrons, disappointed at the loss of old card catalogs, must admit that electronic walking is something that can be achieved only through an OPAC system.

Word Search Techniques

Quick search is a CARL option that saves you from returning to the beginning of the search program each time you want to start a new search. A quick search can be executed from any screen by entering commands in a special format. Briefly stated, you tell the system to do an immediate search by typing:

```
176 Martin Mick                                    MONT
      Video movie guide : 1989                     791.43M382V1989

177 Marx Groucho                                   MONT                  1976
      Grouchophile                                 791.43M3915M

178 Anobile Richard J                              MONT                  1971
      Why a duck?  Visual and verbal gems from the Mar 791.43M392A

179 Adamson Joe                                    MONT                  1973
      Groucho, Harpo, Chico - And Sometimes Zeppo  791.43M392AD

180 Marx Samuel 1902                               MONT                  1987
      A gaudy spree :   the literary life of Hollywood 791.43M3922G

181 Mast Gerald 1940                               MONT                  1973
      The comic mind;   comedy and the movies.     791.43M423C

182 Mast gerald 1940                               MONT                  1971
      Short history of the movies                  791.43M423S

   <RETURN> To continue display
Enter <Line number(s)> To Display Full Records (Number + B  for Brief)
<P>revious For Previous Page OR <Q>uit For New Search
```

FIGURE 4.-9   *OPAC Shelf List* (MCDPL—CARL)

1. Two slash characters (//), indicating a quick search.
2. The initial letter of the kind of search you wish to conduct (W for word, N for name).
3. The term or terms you wish to search for. Note that no space delimits the command letter from the first word. A typical quick search command might look like this:

```
//wcomic*behavior
```

The first letter of the type of search selected (w for word) immediately precedes the first search term (comic*).

You can narrow a search by date, specifying before (<year), after (>year), or a range with first and last years connected by an underscore (_). Thus depression >1929 would look for all entries with the key word depression, and published after 1929; `jazz 1920_1925` would bring out listings covering the jazz age from 1920 to 1925.

Can you imagine the list you would get if you searched for UNITED STATES HISTORY? Don't forget to make your search more specific and reduce the size of the list by adding another word to your search. The result will be citations in your current list that also contain the new word. If your search produces more items than you wish to view at once, you can refine it and eliminate many unwanted items by adding terms. Narrow a word or name search by specifying one or more document types (formats): book, series, article, film, sound recording, juvenile, biography, etc. Or include Boolean delimiters: `marx biography and not karl`

Other Search Techniques

Most OPAC systems include Help functions to explain additional syntax that may apply to some commands. Try typing the command preceded or followed by a question mark, or typing it without any qualification while on the main screen. Before composing a Boolean search string, run a test to see what capability is available. When working with an unfamiliar library, I test it out by entering a word search for the following: `female writers and 1900_1996 and biography and not poet*`

The wild card allows extensions causing the search to match poetical, poets, and poetry. The probability of a hit on that lengthy a specification may be low, but in the process the string tests several functions. The response should show the extent of searching capability. First, it may be necessary to segment the request. Some systems combine two or three words in a single search, then allow added words in subsequent searches. The system may convert 1900_1996 to 20TH

CENTURY. All that says is that it understands dates. If all goes well, I should find a biography of Virginia Woolf listed, but would not see the nineteenth-century author, Mary Shelley. A cross-check on names would reveal whether anything about the authors is on record. Enter common numbers both as letters and as numerals to increase the probability of hits; 12, twelve, and dozen, for instance. Remember, you don't know how the person originally composing the record keyed it in. If known, ISBN numbers entered as digits can be helpful in finding paperback, hardback, and foreign language editions.

Sometimes short stories, plays, speeches, songs, etc., are contents of larger works such as anthologies. The best way to find them would be through a Word search. Word searches look into the descriptors of Contents, Other Entries, and Extra Notes.

You may get a broader electronic listing than what is available on the shelves. Some library systems allow you to investigate the status of individual holdings—location by branch, in or out, on order, reference only, etc. (Figure 4-8). Use this facility prior to any visit to borrow books known to be in the collection.

Other OPAC Systems

You will probably want to investigate OPAC systems other than CARL. Unfortunately, there is little uniformity among them. Each one has its own command language and menu structure, some unique to the library supporting them. Most were developed by computer science departments as part of university campuswide information systems (CWIS). Some, like the system at the Library of Congress, grew out of hard-wired mainframe applications, and were rewritten to adapt to a wider Internet clientele. Standardization is sparse, and in any event, funding for such campuswide information systems redesign is hard to find. Libraries are inclined to stay with invested efforts that already serve most of their regular users. How then can others poke around in distant and unfamiliar online catalogs?

Hope lies in the fact that there is a standard MARC, MAchine Readable Catalog record format, developed by the Library of Congress, defined by the American National Standards Institute (ANSI), and used by most libraries.[1] It's best to become familiar with the use of one OPAC and make the transition to another by compiling a syntax "cheat-sheet" for the necessary searching and display commands. OPAC command structures can be defined in six categories, with many variations. Keep these in mind as you look for the commands that walk you through the system and invoke the MARC descriptors.

Command types encountered in normal sequence are as follows:

1. Navigational—logging in, moving forward or backward within menus, invoking Help screens, exiting gracefully
2. Searching—submission of various search element types for matching against MARC indexes; e.g., author, title, key word, classification code, media type
3. Logical—wild cards, truncation/extension of commands and key words, use of Boolean control words
4. Limiting factors—dates, language, collections (e.g., juvenile, foreign, prints and photographs, serials)
5. Display—short or extended citation, enumerated or single item presentation, screen or printed output
6. Miscellaneous—special features unique to the OPAC

system, such as editing, retracing or recalling earlier searches, timing out upon a period of inactivity
(with or without warning). Some systems, like CARL,
are gateways to others and either handle the pass-
through by imposing their own command language
(doing the translation for you), or warning that you
are stepping into new command territory.

Using a spreadsheet program or word processor, draw up
a columnar search guide such as shown in Table 4-1, or copy
the page, and use it to record your observations as you pro-
ceed.

For doing extended searching through unfamiliar OPAC
systems, you will find *Search Sheets for OPACs on the Internet*
to be useful. The authors have developed a standard method
of describing OPAC menus and search commands, which
they use to describe the commands and prompts of the major
catalog systems. Its tables are more detailed than described
above; they make up your "cheat-sheets" for you. Using it to
speed up distant searches on the Internet may avoid the frustration of being disconnected for excessive delay in issuing
commands. That usually happens just before you find the
right key to retrieve twenty rare and useful citations.

Journals and Periodicals

Online catalogs, at best, describe the existence of a library's
serial holdings. They don't list magazine content. A visit to
the periodical section will give you an idea of the extent of a
library's periodical and professional journal collection. You
can find what publications are on the subscription list, and
how far back the holdings extend. Since periodicals are

Table 4-1 OPAC Search Guide

OPAC System			
Category	Command	Search by/for	Example
Navigational		login forward/back Help exit	
Searching		author title keyword classification media	
Logical		wild cards Boolean	
Limiting factors		date, collections, etc.	
Display		citation formats; presentation formats	
Miscellaneous			

among the most popular resources, the library is always the first place to look when searching for a specific article or topic. Examine recent issues of *Readers' Guide to Periodical Literature* (available in CD-ROM and online in some libraries as well as in print) or similar publications, and go from there. This is the most straightforward method to find and copy any article of recent interest. If you come up short—perhaps the older holdings were purged or the desired issue is missing— or you just can't get to the facility, you have an online solution in UnCover. You can reach this commercial operation by direct dialing (data connection, not voice), by telnet, or through an affiliated CARL system. (See Appendix A for contact details.)

You can browse the UnCover (http://www.carl.org/) catalog with its millions of full-text articles and read many articles online without charge. Others may be ordered for delivery at generally reasonable fees. In preparation for your call, you should have your credit card or account number nearby and your fax program configured to receive. If you will be ordering articles frequently or don't care to give your credit card number over a phone line, you can arrange in advance to open a deposit account.

An Online Journal Search

To include something a little more learned in my study of the Marx Brothers, a journal search might do the trick. After working with a CARL public access catalog, the commands should be familiar. UnCover menus coach you in using the CARL search commands (W, N, B) as explained above.

Here I have used a quick search command for my topic to show a variant of the command structure (Figure 4-10). This

```
                           Welcome to
                            UnCover
              The Article Access and Delivery Solution

  UnCover contains records describing journals and their contents.  Over
  4000 current citations are added daily.  UnCover offers you the opportunity
  to order fax copies of articles from this database.

  To use UnCover, enter:     W  for  WORD or TOPIC search
                             N  for  AUTHOR search
                             B  to   BROWSE by journal title

  For information, type:      ?  to learn about UnCover
                             ?C to learn about UnCover Complete
                             ?R to learn about UnCover Reveal ALERT service
                             QS to learn about searching short-cuts
  To leave UnCover, type:     S  to STOP or SWITCH to another database

  Type the letter(s) of the UnCover service you want and press <RETURN>
                    SELECTED DATABASE:  UnCover

  ENTER  COMMAND (use  //EXIT  to return HOME)>>      //wmarx brothers
```

FIGURE 4-10   UnCover *Introductory Menu* (UnCover Company)

is useful when in the middle of an ongoing search, as I might have been when connected to my local library.

Two articles were found, and I selected the more recent

FIGURE 4-11   UnCover *Search Results* (UnCover)

```
  WORKING...
  MARX    425 ITEMS         UnCover
  MARX + BROTHERS     2 ITEMS

  Set of 2 will display on one page -- proceeding with display...

  ALL ITEMS ARE BEING DISPLAYED.
    1 Lieberfeld, Daniel                      (The american scholar.   Wint 85 )
        Here Under False Pretenses: The Marx Brothers Crash

    2 Haas, Scott                                  (Cineaste.   1992    )
        The Marx Brothers, Jews, and My Four-Year-Old Daught...

   <RETURN> to CONTINUE, Number + M (ex. 3M) to MARK article
  Enter <Line numbers> to see FULL records
  <P>revious for PREVIOUS page,<Q>uit for NEW search
```

```
--------------------------------------------------UnCover--------------------
AUTHOR(s):      Lieberfeld, Daniel
                Sanders, Judith
TITLE(s):       Here Under False Pretenses: The Marx Brothers Crash the
                Gates.

         In:    The american scholar.
                Wint 1995 v 64 n 1
      Page:     103
  SICI Code:    0003-0937(199521)64:1L.103:HUFP;1-

OWNERS: AUR CSU CU  DPL DU  LUT UNC

ISSUE STATUS: Published

This article may be available in your library, at no cost to you.  To have
   it faxed from UnCover, the following charges apply:

Service Charge:   $    6.50
more follows -- press <RETURN> (Q to quit)_
```

FIGURE 4-12   UnCover *Citation* (UnCover)

one to investigate details. With this information I could return to my own library's periodical collection if it carries *The American Scholar*, or order a fax delivery of the article online. (That's a Phi Beta Kappa journal—everybody loves Groucho.) Two phone lines aren't necessary for limited use of a computer-based fax program with online inquiries; just alternate the functions, using the same communications port as your terminal emulation program; probably one program serves both purposes.

First, with the fax function stopped, connect to UnCover through the terminal emulator. Articles selected display a breakdown of the charges for copyright fee and fax delivery. Follow the prompts to mark and order desired items. Hang up, end terminal emulation, and start your fax in receive mode. UnCover takes from a few minutes to twenty-four hours to find the articles and initiate the fax transmission. If it encounters a not-ready situation, it makes several retries. You are charged only for what is delivered. After the faxes are filed

```
* AUTHOR(s):      Maltin, Leonard.
TITLE(s):         The great movie comedians: from Charlie Chaplin to Woody
                  Allen (New York: Crown Publishers, c1978).
                  xvii, 238 p. : ill. ;  26 cm.
CALL #: 791.43092 M26162
* AUTHOR(s):      Marx, Maxine.
TITLE(s):         Growing up with Chico (Englewood Cliffs, N.J.: Prentice-Hall,
   c1980).
                  ix, 181 p., [8] leaves of plates: ill.; 24 cm. Index
CALL #: BM3878M
* AUTHOR(s):      Marx, Groucho,  1891-1977.
TITLE(s):         The Marx Bros. scrapbook, by Groucho Marx and Richard J.
                  Anobile.(New York [Darien House];distributed by Norton,1973).
                  256 p. illus. 29 cm.
CALL #: PN2297.M3M3
* AUTHOR(s):      Adamson, Joe.
TITLE(s):         Groucho, Harpo, Chico, and sometimes Zeppo; a history of
                  the Marx Brothers and a satire on the rest of the world.
                  (New York,  Simon and Schuster  [1973]).
                  464 p. illus. 23 cm.
                  Bibliography: p. 447-451.
CALL #: PN2297.M3A4
* AUTHOR(s):      Eyles, Allen.
TITLE(s):         The Marx brothers; their world of comedy.[2d ed.]
                  (New York,  A. S. Barnes  [1969]).
                  176 p.  illus. 16 cm.
                  Bibliography: p. 173-176.
CALL #:  ?
* AUTHOR(s):      Gehring, Wes D.
TITLE(s):         The Marx brothers: a bio-bibliography (New York:Greenwood
   Press, 1987).
                  xv, 262 p. :  ill. ;  25 cm. Index.
                  Bibliography: p. [214]-225.
                  Filmography: p. [239]-244.
                  Discography: p. [245]-246.
CALL #: PN2297.M3G44 1987
* AUTHOR(s):      Zimmerman, Paul D.
TITLE(s):         The Marx Brothers at the movies / by Paul D. Zimmerman and
                  Burt Goldblatt. (New York: New American Library,1968)
   262 p. :  ill., ports. ;  19 cm.
CALL #: PN2297.M3Z5 1968a
* AUTHOR(s):      Lieberfeld, Daniel
                  Sanders, Judith
TITLE(s):         Here Under False Pretenses: The Marx Brothers Crash the
                  Gates.
         In:      The american scholar.
                  Wint 1995 v 64 n 1
       Page:      103
* AUTHOR(s):      Haas, Scott
TITLE(s):         The Marx Brothers, Jews, and My Four-Year-Old Daughter.
         In:      Cineaste.
                  1992 v 19 n 2 / 3
       Page:      48
```

FIGURE 4-13 *Preliminary Master List*

in your computer, you can read or print them when you want. Since they are graphical files you can't edit or cut-and-paste portions. Remember to add the citations to your master list.

Back to the Library

After preliminary editing of captured screens while doing research on comedians I produced the listing shown in Figure 4-13. This is the beginning of a master list. With it in hand, it is time to go to the local library. An actual visit to the stacks can give you an idea of the popularity of your topic, at least in that location. Observe the due dates stamped on the back of the books for an indication of how frequently and in what period the books have been borrowed. I once found a set of books on an interesting topic—library research. All were over five years old and most had been withdrawn in recent months. I suspected this to be a sign the subject matter was both popular and in need of updating. That suggested there was a market for the topic, started me on extended research, and led me to write the book you are now reading.

5
Searching on the Internet

Encyclopedia articles and CD-ROM references provide basic information. Delving into OPACs brings you no deeper than the title pages of books and recording jackets. Online journal searching helps you review the content of magazines and professional journals, and sometimes get complete articles.

The next area to search is the Internet. There you can plumb the minds of people you have never met and probably never will. Or better, lurk unidentified, "listening in" as these people discuss an enormous variety of issues. You can examine hundreds of specialized articles and the content of many statistical databases, get descriptions of museum exhibits and directions, even street maps telling how to go there. Haven't had much experience on the Net? You could take a six-week course, free, online. (See Patrick Crispen's Roadmap in Appendix A.) Hundreds of guide books on using the Internet can be found in bookstores. My favorites are in the bibliography to get you started or extend your knowledge. The

Internet can be overwhelming without an introduction to its facilities. This chapter does that with an overview on hunting for information. Information on participating in forums or contributing information can be found in a multitude of other texts available about the Net, and therefore, have not been included here.

The Major Internet Applications

Hundreds of applications are used daily on the Internet. People play chess in real time across international borders, they check the contents of vending machines, teach classes, take attendance, and give exams. Most activities are variations of six common applications, each valuable in a different way for gathering information: mail exchange, remote server connection, file transfer, and searching by context, key word, and cross-reference.

Nine variations of these six applications are discussed here in the order of their value as information sources from the most direct and simplest to the richest and most fruitful. Functionally, this is what they offer:

E-mail—electronic message exchange
Newsgroups—topical bulletin boards
Mailing lists—special interest group subscriptions
Telnet—read-and-copy connection to remote servers
FTP—receipt of files from archival sites
Gopher—directory searching within context
Archie—archived directory searching by keyword
WAIS—logical keyword searching within texts
WWW—directory and file searching by cross-reference.

You will see how SLIP-based applications simplify your research efforts, while learning how to get most of the graphical benefits of SLIP accounts (see "Technical Details: Your Internet connection" in chapter 1, page 8) without incurring extra periodic charges. The World Wide Web (WWW) is the major attraction, and you may be tempted to jump right into it and try it out. It *is* a lot of fun. There are two good reasons why you should try to understand the more basic applications, and experiment with some in the sequence presented. First, if you master text-based e-mail, newsgroups, and mailing lists you will be able to find your way economically to a large population of people with more interest in trading information than in selling things. Second, by exploring the mid-range applications (telnet and Gopher, perhaps also FTP) you will gain a better appreciation for functions that support advanced use of the WWW. Familiarity breeds respect. Eventually, you are likely to find that while WWW is fun to explore, telnet and mailing lists provide a more consistent supply of useful information.

E-Mail

The original and most commonly used Net application is message exchange, handled through several programs available as part of all service provider subscriptions. You can compose and send messages to individuals or to remote computers, and receive, store, and forward messages sent to you. A standard text-based message structure assures compatibility between all systems and programs. Macintosh, Unix, DOS, Windows, and OS/2 users can exchange messages while unaware of each other's terminal type. The addressing structure is always in this form:

```
userid@system.organization.type
```

What is probably of most interest is the last term, which tells you what type of organization (see below) is the owner of the address. Non-U.S. e-mail addresses indicate the country, for example, an e-mail address ending in .uk is British.

.com—commercial supplier, such as compuserve.com
.edu—educational site, such as k12.ucs.umass.edu
.gov—government, such as whitehouse.gov
.mil—military, such as nctamslant.navy.mil
.net—network servicer/ISP, such as digex.net
.org—non-profit organizations, such as cpcug.org

E-mail programs offer a wide range of sophistication. Your service provider should make recommendations and equip you with necessary manuals or pointers to online Help screens. E-mail operation consists of opening new mail, composing and sending messages, and maintenance of a personal file of commonly used Internet addresses under more familiar nicknames. Mail is held in storage repositories called baskets, folders or boxes; the terminology varies. E-mail is useful for corresponding with known information resources such as PROFNET, subscribing to listservs, and privately contacting people who have posted to newsgroups or lists.

Newsgroups

There are thousands and thousands of Internet newsgroups, most having nothing to do with current world or local events. You don't get that kind of news. The groups are organized on

Usenet, which may be envisioned as a virtual subnetwork of the Internet (refer to Figure 1-1 on page 8), and administered by UUNET Technologies Inc. (uunet.uu.net) and many volunteers. Newsgroups are the bulletin boards of the Internet, specialized in content, some for discussion, others for queries or announcements, established under Usenet protocols, and controlled mostly by contributors' interests. There are organizational rules for posting to newsgroups and suggestions for proper online behavior (called "netiquette"), but minimal policing. Some newsgroups may be moderated, meaning that articles/messages are submitted through a person responsible for keeping postings on target and acceptable, but there is little censorship. Most bulletin boards are wide open for posting from anyone about anything. First Amendment rights are hotly defended by Net users. The Communications Decency Act had little impact on newsgroup content, so be prepared for just about anything.

When you travel to a foreign country where you might find people driving on the "wrong" side of the road, removing their shoes before entering a house, or complimenting the cook with a burp, while bemused by the cultural differences, you wouldn't scoff at them. So, too, with the world of the Net. You'll encounter a different culture, born in Defense Department research labs, nurtured in the halls of academe, exploited in college dormitories, and now attracting ordinary citizens worldwide with its milieu of opinions, trivia, and sometimes valuable information.

Certain newsgroups probably become available to you by default at login, typically ones with `help` and `answers` in their titles. Usenet classifies newsgroups according to topical content, qualified further by purpose. Among them you will find these first-level classifications:

alt.   Alternate interests, a large "catchall" set of groups open to anyone for anything.

comp.   Computers, another large list covering every aspect of computer philosophy, hardware, software, design, and use.

news.   Not daily current events, but news about Usenet and the newsgroup organization.

rec.   Recreational matter, games, humor, performing arts, music.

sci.   Scientific. What the Internet was first developed for, covers anything in the hard sciences.

soc.   Social sciences, liberal arts; cultural matters, history, religion, etc.

There are many more beyond that. Within titles, subsequent classification words narrow the topics further. The final word sometimes qualifies the content for specific Usenet purposes (.announce,.help,.important,.news, etc.). Posting to those is prohibited except through e-mail to authorized moderators. You should be aware that messages posted to newsgroups are often archived, and what you wrote can be searched and located with your name or userid attached to it.

Your Internet service provider probably offers a choice of text-based newsreader programs. Newsgroups deal mostly with relatively small text files, and you can get started exploring them using only your communications program and whatever software your ISP makes available on the server without having to buy or install anything extra. But for ease of use, a graphical newsreader installed on your computer is preferable. You'll find them for Macintosh, Windows, and OS/2, included with the more popular Internet navigators discussed below in the section on browsers.

In selecting a newsreader from your ISP's menu, consider

another criterion: Do you want to read postings in the order they arrive at the newsgroup, or logically arranged by topic? "Hot" topics, those of wide current interest or considered controversial by the newsgroup constituents, usually result in a series of follow-up responses, and responses to responses. Postings are called articles, and a series of articles on the same subject is called a thread. Within a newsgroup, other articles might arrive for posting between hot topic responses. Some newsreaders present the articles in order received, leaving it to you to trace threads by mentally sorting in subject sequence. Others automatically group threads under the lead article. If you don't follow a newsgroup regularly you might prefer a chronological listing.

Controversial newsgroups are better examined in threaded order. Three text-based versions of commonly available news-

FIGURE 5-1 *NewsReader Article Listing* (Credit Usenet Inc., the original authors of ABOI, alt.best.of.internet, Malinda McCall and Onno Benschop, and current ABOI editor, Jon Abbott. Listing delivered using the Tin newsreader, copyright 1993, Iain Lea, Nuremberg, Germany)

```
  49  + 14 Free Agent                                 Steve
  50  +     THIS IS A TEST
  51  +     Children's Christian Church Answers        M. Medenis
  52  + 9   ???WHERE IS THE BEST SERVICE PROViDER ON THE  Paul Seaton
  53  + 6   FREE Internet Access!!                      Nicholas
  54  +     FREE Zip programmes to download-Description. abba@gil.ipswichci
  55  +     Open News Server                            Joe
  56  +     personal home pages!                        mking@ns1.koyote.c
  57  + 2   Women and employers are alike              Patrick Costello
  58  +     ABOI: Barbie Explosions                     Russell Bramley
  59  + 2   Run Over neighbors cat                      Arthur Calhoun
  60  +     Best newsgroup reader                       Robert Tasse
  61  +     IBM 360/30 saga (long)                      Stewart Stremler
  62  + 2   an urban legend sighted in a poem by ellen ba David Gerard
  63  +     ABOI: TROTSKY talks, like, to the YOUTH!!   Malinda McCall
  64  +     Salvador Dali Tour Online!                  Carl I. Merchant

 <n>=set current to n, TAB=next unread, /=search pattern, ^K)ill/select,
a)uthor search, c)atchup, j=line down, k=line up, K=mark read, l)ist thread,
 |=pipe, m)ail, o=print, q)uit, r=toggle all/unread, s)ave, t)ag, w=post
```

readers are RN (sometimes called ReadNews) which lists current articles chronologically, TRN (Threaded ReadNews), and Tin (Threaded Internet News, perhaps), delivering threaded article lists.[2] All are similar, with tightly structured keystroke commands, briefly described on a screen-wide menu in sometimes arcane language. You can avoid this by using a friendlier graphical interface.

Newsgroup Housekeeping

Newsgroups can be investigated on a one-time basis, like buying a newsstand copy of a magazine, or unread articles can be delivered routinely by subscription. Certain newsgroups warrant a subscription to keep informed about Usenet itself. When you are familiar with the process you can selectively evaluate and add more newsgroups to your subscription list. Subscribing is done through a simple procedure:

1. Your account service probably includes reading newsgroups in its menu of options. The first time you invoke this choice you are presented with a very long list, thousands of entries. Subscribed-to groups, if any, are listed first, in subscription order. The others follow in alphabetical order, the alt. groups near the top of the list. Ignore most entries until you get your subscription defaults established. You can examine the full list later to extend your understanding of newsgroup organization. There is even a quick method available through the Web for finding pertinent newsgroups. Newsreaders keep records on your activities. On subsequent calls for newsgroups you will be presented first with a list of those generated since your last session and the option to subscribe to

each. New ones are invented with alarming frequency. You'll soon learn to q)uit or Esc)ape from this query, as it interferes with your primary purpose.

2. Look in the command guide for the search key (possibly /=search pattern), and others to s)ubscribe and u)nsubscribe. With the cursor at the command line, search for news by entering /news.*

3. After a few seconds you should see the middle of the list with the cursor pointing to the first news. entry. Using the cursor control keys, select and s)ubscribe to each of the following:

```
news.announce.important
news.announce.newusers
news.answers
news.newusers.questions
```

The first three were described in chapter 3. We haven't talked about the fourth but it will be helpful to have available for a short period after you subscribe. When you find you can answer most of the questions, it's a simple matter to u)nsubscribe.

4. Key in the command to quit, causing your selections to be filed, then re-issue the read newsgroups command. The initialization process puts your subscriptions at the top of the list.

After that the process becomes habitual. Using the newsreader, select subscribed newsgroups for review; select unread articles of interest from the list of headings; read; quit. Take time to read every article in the first two groups. The newsreader keeps a list in storage of identifiers of articles read and discarded. Normally you would not see those again. Articles remain in newsgroups for periods that depend on the volatility of the group, the policy of the moderator, and the administrator of the service machine. The first two groups won't change much, whereas the articles in news.answers are many and lengthy, remaining listed only for a day or two before removal. It is here that newsgroup owners post official notices about their groups. The files contain answers to Frequently Asked Questions (FAQs) for the respective group—How do I find something? What does some word or phrase mean? FAQs are updated periodically by an experienced newsgroup subscriber and posted regularly to news.answers.

Within a month, you will find most of the popular FAQs have cycled through the posting process. People learn on the Net by reading FAQs. Do the same thing during your first month of Internet connection. You'll soon learn to scan the listings rapidly, looking for key words. Pick out those of interest, read the FAQs (some may be worth saving in your file space for later reference and study), and subscribe if the newsgroup seems interesting. Start by scanning FAQs of interest when they show up in news.answers. Later in this chapter you will see how to retrieve archived FAQs—those that have been posted and removed from the current release of the newsgroup.

As helpful as they can be, you can also waste an inordinate amount of time with newsgroups. Unless you compulsively read magazines and newspapers cover-to-cover, you will probably be selective in reading listed articles. Open those of interest, read and quit. The article is marked to exclude it from subsequent lists unless additional threaded articles are appended. When you reselect the lead article in the thread you should be served the first unread article. Upon completing your review of the newsgroup, a command can mark all listed articles as read and to be discarded. Should you quit without using it, the unread articles will still be listed upon your return.

Using Internet Newsgroups

Try to become sensitive to the characteristics of newsgroup followers. The medium itself acts as a filter. You might assume subscribers to be literate and somewhat technical since, like you, they are conversant with computers.

The best way to size up your unseen network comrades is the practice of "lurking." Follow threads of interest, but don't be quick to join in. Gradually you will develop a sense of the crowd's traits. You may find that the "crowd" consists of a few electronic gossips with time on their hands and little potential for your needs. Then it's time to move on.

Listservs

Gateway connections make the distinction vague between different networks. A subset of the Internet, BITNET is an international research-and-education network (illustrated in Figure 1-1 on page 8) made up of 2,300 organizations supporting e-mail, File Transfer Protocol (FTP), and several mailing list servers, most running the Unix-based program ListServ. Many mailing list names typically start with bit.list serv, followed by a descriptive word (bit.listserv.edtech,bit. listserv.history, etc.). That's usually a clue to the list originating in a university or research organization. Many have different first-level names, often with -L appended (e.g., MARHST-L is a maritime history list) and use a variety of similar programs: ListProc, Majordomo, and others. Wherever located, all list servers do essentially the same things—receive rigidly formatted e-mail to add (subscribe) or remove (unsubscribe) user addresses in mailing lists and receive and distribute articles, some with a moderator, who approves subscribers and article content first. Programs differ enough in their operation that there is not a consistent approach to their usage.

Mailing lists are introduced and re-announced periodically through newsgroups. FAQs explain how to subscribe. Details can also be found in *The Internet Directory* and *The Internet Yellow Pages*. E-mail subscription requests are read by programs, not usually by people. Once on a mailing list you may find your mail reader regularly inundated by largely uninteresting messages. Important: before subscribing, make note of exactly how to unsubscribe or pause mail delivery. Look for the welcome message customarily delivered with a new subscription; it should explain how to unsubscribe. For some reason, the unsubscribing process is apt to be fussier than the subscribing process.

The article content delivered through a mailing list differs from that of a newsgroup devoted to the same subject. It is less interactive, more specialized, often moderated, and may contain long "white papers" similar to journal articles. People with singular interests find this to be the major advantage of a mailing list. Let a subscription run for a while to decide if it's the right thing for you.

Telnet

Telnet allows you to use remote systems as if you are directly connected to them. Your own node becomes transparent as you pass through to a telnet host. You log in to the remote system in the customary manner with an appropriate user name and password. Some hosts require that you have a prearranged account, such as you have with your own service provider. Other hosts allow anyone to log in, either as "anonymous," "guest" or with a userid provided in the opening screen.

In these cases the proper response to the password prompt is your fully qualified Internet address (userid@ domain), or you may just press the Enter key, giving no password. You won't know what works until you try it, unless you have unearthed specifics from books like *The Internet Directory*. Anonymous users can only read and copy files. Some anonymous-telnet sites expect a numerical value identifying a login port to be given as part of the target address. It channels users to suitably coded support for their computer environment. By common convention, default guest ports are often 23 or 80.

The term telnet specifies a protocol, a client-server set of programs, and a Unix command. As a protocol it defines how the TCP/IP process handles data transmission between local and remote sites. The term is often used as a verb: "telnet to locis.loc.gov" for instance, to get Library of Congress information. It is through telnet that vending machines (servers) inform users (clients) about their contents. Information seekers telnet to OPACs for library catalogs, and to online databases for weather reports, stock market averages, historical documents, government statistics, geographic data, telephone directories and many other useful files. You may want to keep notes of your favorite telnet discoveries for later reference. Evaluate them for accessibility, port requirements, ease of use, and material content. That's a practical use of the index cards discussed in chapter 4.

Invoking telnet at your service machine is simplicity itself; interacting with the remote end may not be. After connection to your service provider, shift to the Unix command line. The

Unix prompt is usually the percent symbol (%). Some systems change that to the classic DOS prompt (>), or their own option (! or ?). Key in the command `telnet`, followed by the address of the target site. After giving a valid target address you should receive a progress message that the client program on your end is "Trying" followed by the IP address of the remote site, then after connecting to the server site, a second message reports "Connected to" the site's Internet name. Follow these messages carefully for connection information.

Following the escape-sequence message you should get the prompt `telnet>` as the server waits for your command. You are on your way with the login sequence, and can judge the accessibility and friendliness of the remote facility by what is displayed on subsequent screens. Some are quite user-friendly, anticipating needs and ready with Help screens on request. Most OPACs are that way. Other sites respond as if they were intended only for a few knowing insiders. If you find that to be the case, it may be best to just move on.

File Transfer (FTP)

Its real name is file transfer protocol. Everyone calls it FTP, a utility belonging in the domain of the Internet guru. Suppose you discover names of files you want to copy because of things you read in newsgroups or in telnet-displayed documents. In browsing long FAQs of potential interest, the beginning or end of the files may have details on how to get the FAQ later by FTP. Many FAQs are archived at a site with an interesting name rtfm.mit.edu. I mentioned in the introduction that MIT was worth a visit, but I'll leave it to you to decode the rest (see Glossary, Appendix B). A computer at MIT is an archival repository for most of the Usenet FAQs. Hundreds of other archives exist around the world, with programs, pictures, prose, and poetry available for the effort of using FTP.

Get started with FTP much as you did with telnet, at the Unix prompt entering "FTP" followed by the target address. Upon successful connection, the response will be the prompt FTP>, and the target server waits for your command. That's the easy part. You will need your service provider's manual for step-by-step procedures to go from there. FTP is not for everyone. The nature of digging through strange directory structures to retrieve files from unfamiliar hosts makes it cumbersome. Often you would do better to turn on your data capture program and read files of interest when you first encounter them. But don't let your interest flag—there are other methods for getting the information, as we will see next.

Navigators

As you become familiar with resources on the Net, you will sense that there are untapped riches out there in the electronic world that must be investigated. Newsgroups give you ideas, telnet and FTP get you closer, but they hit targets broadside when you may want a well-placed rifle shot. Those key words you so carefully compiled have hardly been exercised at this point. Notations on index cards have only increased your intellectual avarice. In this state you need a navigator—something that lets you run down any pathway, looking in windows and doors, tracking where you've been, where you are and then points to where you might want to go next. The first navigators were text-based. I'll talk more about these in the next section, Other Internet Applications. Later navigators added graphical user interfaces and multitasking, culminating in Netscape, the most popular navigator for exploring the Web, and described under the topic of Browsers.

Other Internet Applications:
Gopher, Archie, and WAIS

Gopher, a text-based client-server application, tunnels through the Net (one reason for the name[4]), linking menu-driven databases at your command until you arrive at documents of interest. All you need is access to any one of the hundreds of Gopher servers around the world, then you can travel to any of the others merely by selecting menu items. Any full ser-vice provider either operates a Gopher server or links to one transparently at the gopher command. You get access to ei-ther a menu, an index, a telnet connection, or a document. Narrowing your search, you select likely targets from topic listings while something under the covers telnets you to an-other server. If at any time, a menu or index doesn't appear to be what you need, just back out and try another selection from the previous menu. Finally, like journal searches in Un-Cover (chapter 4), you arrive at the identification of the docu-ment you want. Select it and gopher code under the covers gets it for you, popping it into your home site's editor. A few pages will arrive in seconds. Long documents, like some FAQs, may take minutes.

Here is a log of what I did to collect information on the key words "pediatric inoculation statistics." This technique is called context searching. Note that I didn't use any of those words, except in my mind.

7:50 P.M.   Dialed, connected and logged in to cpcug.org, my home site.

7:51 P.M.   Selected Gopher from the shell menu, and option 5, Other Gophers of Interest.

7:52 P.M.   Option 2, Gopher JEWELS (University of Southern California). "Jewels" are lists of interesting topics, usually a good starting choice.

7:53 P.M.   Option 7, Health, Medical, Disability.

7:54 P.M.   Option 3, Medical Related.

7:54 P.M.   Next menu option 3, Medical Related (misc.), an extension.

7:55 P.M.   Option 28 (second page), Maternal and Child (MCH-Net).

7:55 P.M.   Option 11, Child Health Data.

7:56 P.M.   Option 6, Vaccination—2 Yr Olds, a document.

7:57 P.M.   After scanning two pages, Print.

Seconds later I had the full Centers for Disease Control paper, prepared two months earlier, in my hands.

There are only a few key-commands needed to work through any menu, similar to those in newsreaders. For text files, there is little more to tell you about Gopher, it is that straightforward. Binary files (images, programs, sound) can also be retrieved. Much more computing power is needed to make use of them, and currently they remain in the novelty category, hardly extending the frontiers of knowledge. Our approach has been to describe the most economical text-mode uses of the Internet, providing probably 90 percent of available useful information. We'll not cover the process of retrieving pretty pictures and background music with Gopher. But, as I've said before, stay tuned.

Where Gopher presents directory listings in which you narrow the context to your interests, Archie is the inverse, going directly to archival sites to look for key word matches. Give it key words representing what's on your mind, and it attempts to match the strings with the descriptive names of archived files. It can find and retrieve both text and binary files, working from a database of FTP archive sites and registered Internet resource owners.

Another searching tool is the client-server package Wide-Area Information Server (WAIS). In WAIS everything presented is an index from which you select documents that look pertinent. WAIS takes key words as search elements, analyzes the relevance of everything it finds, and presents an indexed and weighted list of titles or headlines found. Elements can include Boolean search terms. The frequency of occurrence of each term within a full-text search establishes the potential success of the search, expressed as a parenthetical "score" in the listing. You'll see evidence of WAIS activity when you use WWW searching mechanisms.

World Wide Web

The next information searching requirement is for cross-referencing. Printed encyclopedias lead you to cross-referenced articles with words capitalized or in bold type. Computers use hypertext to do the same thing. WWW links Gopher-type servers and documents with hypertext. Behind the scenes, hypertext mark-up language (HTML) links cross-references highlighted within the text. Files are then sent to requesters' sites under hypertext transmission protocol (HTTP). The program handling the interaction is called a browser, and with one exception, must be resident in your own machine. It leans heavily on internal telnet, gopher, and FTP functions to get things done. Hypertext sets the direction of each search, directory-by-directory. From some arbitrary starting point you can trace any route you'd care to, back up, or jump to a previous route, hence the significance of the term "web." Entries in a directory might represent local files or subdirectories, or they might point to other Web sites anywhere in the world. Linking furnishes the navigator that takes you around. A browser formats incoming data streams for textual and graphical presentation. Some of the popular browsers and a valuable extension are reviewed below. Refer to Appendix A for the sources from which they may be obtained.

Browsers

Lynx, the only browser not installed on the user's computer, is a text-only WWW program for use within regular shell accounts. It can run at lower line speeds, even at 2,400 bps if you are very patient. Most ISPs include it in the standard suite of full service offerings. Some servicers dress the text up with a more colorful user interface. You get no graphics and no mouse-screen interaction. Arrow keys move the cursor to highlighted text, and a few keystrokes execute hypertext activity to jump to the next display. It's a slow process, but it gets you there.

Thus far I have pursued only text-based Internet applications as supplied in shell accounts, cautioning you on the unnecessary expense of graphical support for retrieving essentially text-based information. Browsing the Web with Lynx, no extra code is needed in your terminal for textual data to be delivered to the service provider's computer and out to yours. Terminal emulators display ascii data streams, usually in monochrome, often replete with imbedded icons for control symbols (e.g., ✿), making things a little rough around the edges for the user. Then, too, one must deal with Unix keyed commands, however superficially.

Now let me make life easier, taking you just a few dollars deeper into one-time computer costs, and show you how to access the Internet through Graphical User Interfaces (GUIs), part of Macintosh, Windows and OS/2 operating systems. Faster is definitely better: nearly all Internet service providers can handle 28.8 kbps, or higher, and you can use programs supporting the graphical functions of WWW. This higher level of service requires code installed on your machine's disk. It increases the monthly service cost, even though work is off-loaded from the server to your own computer. However there is a way to get most of the benefits of GUI Web browsers without added SLIP expense—pseudo-SLIP, as it was referred to in chapter 2. But let's start at the beginning.

Lynx is the text-only version of Mosaic, the original graphical Web browser. The latest variants of Mosaic, NCSA Mosaic, produced by the National Center for Computing Applications (NCSA) at the University of Illinois, run with SLIP code installed under Macintosh, Windows, or OS/2. In addition to the browser you can run Gopher, telnet, and a read-only graphical version of newsgroups. E-mail and follow-up messages to newsgroups would be handled through your regular text-based shell account. It was Mosaic that started the explosive growth of WWW activity and gave birth to the idea of cyber-surfing.

Browsing is similar to Gopher searching, in which you narrow the specifications until arriving at a document (Web page) meeting your interest. Web sites are reached through Internet uniform resource locators (URLs) in http format, a combination of protocols and addresses. Some people pronounce the acronym "earl," some say you-are-ell. Newer browsers should contain "Forms" capability to enable interactive submission of requests, and "Mailto" that allows clicking directly on hyperlinked e-mail addresses to send messages while within the browser and specific Web site.

Each Web site has an introductory home page usually containing an index of topics listed in hypertext, possibly a graphic, maybe even sound. Many contain advertising in the form of "banners" that link you to more commercial details, the electronic version of magazine inserts. Hypertext references could link to other directories or files at the current site, or to a URL for something half the world away. The physical locations are of little interest; the topics at the destinations are what capture your imagination.

Routinely in software technology, famous and highly regarded packages are improved to become new and competing products. So it was with Mosaic, the precursor to Netscape Navigator. In 1994, Mosaic Communication Corporation changed its name to Netscape Communications and in the following year released its first product, Netscape Navigator, a competitor to the original and still-evolving Mosaic. Netscape Navigator is a shareware browser; try it without charge, and if satisfied, pay a registration fee. It is usually possible to get Netscape free or bundled with your computer; if you need to buy it, the cost is minimal. It can be downloaded by FTP or directly via your current access to the Web; just click on a Netscape advertising banner when you see it displayed. There are Unix, Macintosh, OS/2, and Windows versions, each requiring a TCP/IP stack in the user's computer, and proprietary server software in the Web sites. Anyone that can manipulate a mouse and read a color display is already trained to use it. In Netscape Navigator you get a user-defined extended history of searches instead of a hot list of URLs, pretty much as easy to work with.

OS/2 Warp provides Internet Access Kit (IAK) as part of its system utilities. IAK contains: SLIP support, Ultimedia Mail/2, NewsReader/2, Telnet, FTP-PM, Gopher, Archie, and Web-Explorer, which is a graphical browser that IBM modeled on Mosaic. These individual programs take advantage of OS/2's multitasking capability and can overlap some of their operations. IAK provides options for automatic connection to IBM's own service provider, Advantis, or dial-up to any other service provider. WebExplorer, the browser, is friendly, fast, and easy to learn, with hot list recording (IBM calls it a quick list). Like Mosaic and Netscape, it keeps the user informed of Web downloading and formatting activity with an animated icon.

Microsoft's Windows 95 browser, Internet Explorer, is built on and competes with earlier versions of Netscape, and like the other browsers includes a newsgroup reader and e-mail handler. In that regard the software is ahead of what most people need or have the hardware to support. As yet the information content of audio and video clips does not come up to what is stocked in traditional technologies by most public libraries. The latest versions of these competing browsers move ahead by simplifying the installation process and offering direct sign-up with a variety of national ISPs.

For dial-up connection, graphical browsers need SLIP/PPP support at the service provider. Some providers arrange single-user SLIP accounts for a one-time setup fee and slightly higher monthly charges. There are new methods to achieve most of the Web graphical functions without SLIP direct connection and its associated cost. Your computer grows beyond terminal capability, differing from true SLIP machines only in reduced graphic/sound-handling speed and inability to perform the customary server functions of fully SLIP-equipped machines. You can only receive files, and cannot share them with others (hence you can't operate a Web site). For infor-

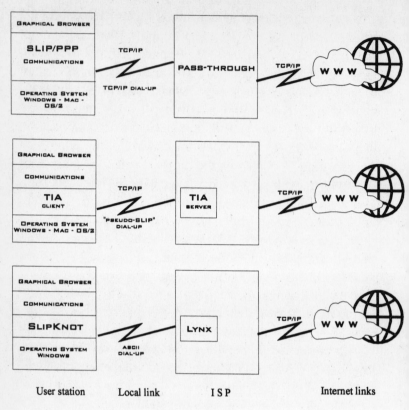

FIGURE 5-2   *Graphical Connections for World Wide Web*

mation seekers these limitations are of little consequence. The small registration fee is usually well justified.

The Internet Adapter (TIA), makes a regular shell account behave much like a SLIP/PPP account. The service provider installs a TIA server as one of its applications and furnishes its dial-up shell users with the appropriate TIA shell interface for their operating system. TIA in the home site has a dual personality: it acts as a server to the user's client terminal, and as a client to remote Web sites.

For users continuing with Windows 3.1, a program called SlipKnot does the work of assembling and unravelling TCP/IP code delivered from a line-mode Web browser like Lynx. It converts the control characters in the data stream to a friendlier display than Lynx normally delivers to a terminal emulator, but, like Lynx itself, this should be considered a temporary approach to Web browsing. More information on these packages will be found in Appendix A. You should also check with your service provider, since matching code must be available in your home site.

Collecting Information From the Web

The Web's job is to link and deliver data, not to store, maintain or present much more than a home page (introductory matter) and, more frequently, innocuous ads that link to commercial sites. The World Wide Web is not a repository, but an efficient pointer to millions of directories and files held in thousands of Internet and peripheral sites. Think of it as the Internet's reference librarian. You can be readily tempted to spend long periods just poking around, cyber-surfing. To suggest that you avoid diversion from anything but a search for project-oriented information would be like sending a kid to the candy store for one M&M. There is much out there that's appealing, a lot that's about as nourishing and good for you as a nougat bar. Your mother would tell you to try to keep focused on what's important in life.

Many Web pages are in effect listings of resources to be found elsewhere, known as subject trees. They are typically made up of topics alphabetically arranged as hypertext pointers (http URLs) to directories and files located just about anywhere on the Net—FTP and gopher sites, archives, other Web documents, etc. Several Web sites got started in the design of catalog-building techniques by automating searches through linked file repositories on the Internet. That led to the development of robots and spiders, known generically as search engines—programs that automatically search Web sites, collecting and indexing URLs by topic, growing nightly as new sites come into being. Like real spiders, they go roaming on the Web when activity is lowest.

World Wide Web Housekeeping

You need to be aware of URLs to find new sites and save them for repeat visits, but thereafter their use is automatic. Most browsers support easy entry of URLs into hot lists for reuse (Lynx uses bookmarks to do the same, Microsoft calls them "favorites," and IBM records them in "quick lists"), avoiding a lot of tedious key entry. Explore the subject trees to get a sense of what is available, as you did when you walked through the reference stacks of the library (chapter 3, The Library, Your Second Office). One reason I suggested in the beginning of this chapter that you first get familiar with the more basic Internet applications is that newsgroups sometimes describe Web sites catering to your interests. When you are ready to collect information the following technique should keep you on target.

1. Keep an external list of the more useful subject trees found (index cards help you categorize them). There are dozens of well-known trees. Some of the more popular ones along with some government Web offerings are listed in the next section.[5] Descriptive comments are based on my own experience. Appendix A explains how to find them.

2. Start a new hot list in your browser with the URL of the first subject tree to be searched. Hot lists tend to collect URLs like closets collect wire coat hangers. You'll need to prune this list from time to time to avoid clutter (see step 5).

3. Explore the subject list, looking for those entries in your field of pursuit. To jump to any page of interest, click on the highlighted hypertext phrase. If it appears suitable, press the key that adds it to the hot list, then return to the subject tree. That takes only a few keystrokes; you do not have to retype long http strings. Browsers' menu bars or icons in well-structured subject trees offer the ability to return to prior pages.

4. Reiterate, adding the next subject tree to the hot list. Multiple references to the same URLs are indicative of popularity or usefulness. Before posting a resource to your hot list, evaluate its suitability for your purposes. Web pages can be published by anyone with SLIP/PPP access and hypertext know-how, and you may discover that this freedom generates some strange ones. A reference to a Web page, even in a well-regarded subject tree, is not testimony to its quality. Furthermore, unlike books, Internet resources are transitory—they can be modified or removed any time. URLs are like phone numbers, subject to change with the owners' circumstances. Some server administrators track the quality and frequency of access to the files they hold, and may purge those that are poorly maintained or in low demand as part of their routine housekeeping activity.

5. When you have exhausted your subject searches, go back and read the resource content. To avoid infor-

mation overload, eliminate hot list references to
pages that appear sparse in content, redundant,
poorly maintained, or of dubious value. Print or copy
to disk currently useful pages, much as you would
photocopy useful reference material in a library. Be
sure to preserve authorship (often expressed with an
e-mail address) and date of publication or update, as
well as the web address (URL), which doesn't always
download with the file. Most browsers allow you to
keep multiple hot lists and move (cut and paste) entries from one position or list to another. It is time
well spent to stay organized.

Some Starting Points

These resources are generally available without charge. Some
carry advertising and presumably survive on the revenue
from that. Others are experimental. Some require registration,
with the implication that fees may be applied later. Searching
with multiple search engines, using the same key words in
each, you will find that quantities and content of identified articles differ. That is because each search engine uses a different technique. Boolean terms required or assumed, frequency
of word occurrence used as a filter, varying proximities of
key words in articles, etc. Thus, it's wise to explore with several. Here are some to start with.

All 4 One (http://www.all4one.com/) An interloper more
than a search engine, it takes advantage of multi-tasking
to initiate four concurrent searches by the more popular
and industrious search machines (AltaVista, Lycos, Yahoo!,
and WebCrawler, all described below). All 4 One requires

Netscape version 2.0 or later, and can detect whether or not you are using it; if not, you are offered a downloaded version for a 90-day no-charge trial.

AltaVista (http://www.altavista.digital.com/) Super search engine that indexes 30 million pages on 225,000 servers, and 3 million articles from 14,000 Usenet newsgroups (statistics as of May 1996). A service of Digital Equipment Corporation, its developers state that it will not fetch pages excluded by webmasters according to Standard for Robot Exclusion (SRE) rules. Although not invoked widely at present, SRE preserves some privacy in a very open environment.

Clearinghouse for Subject-Oriented Internet Resource Guides (http://www.clearinghouse.net/) Argus Associates and the University of Michigan's subject tree takes you deeply into guides to gophers, FTP sites, list servers, and newsgroups in either plain text or HTML versions. Subsets of the guides are organized into humanities, social sciences, and sciences.

c | net inc. (http://www.cnet.com/) Tailor your own search engine with this facility that provides more than 250 ways to search Usenet and the Web. A splendid starting point.

EINet Galaxy (http://www.einet.net/) This search engine lets you set search perimeters within the eleven broad classifications of Galaxy topics, through Gopher sites, Web sites, or combinations of these. Among the Gopher sites threaded to EINet is Gopher Jewels.

Gopher Jewels (http://galaxy.einet.net/GJ/) A useful list of about sixty information categories (subject trees).

InfoSeek (http://www.infoseek.com/) Offers a standard suite of a dozen popular trees, and the ability to search for e-mail addresses, Usenet newsgroups, and stories of events covered in the past month by *Reuters News*.

Inktomi (http://www.inktomi.com/) Part of a project at the University of California at Berkeley, Inktomi takes issue with methods search engines use to count documents, stating that its method of counting the number of documents actually retrieved is the most honest measure of coverage.

Lycos (http://www.lycos.com) Originating at Carnegie Mellon, now the product of Lycos Inc., this is one of the more capable spiders (its name is the shortened form of a species of arachnid). WAIS-type relevance searches are conducted. Two catalogs are maintained, a faster one for searching approximately half a million web pages, and a big one containing at least 5 million web pages and over 37 million URLs.

OpenText (http://index.opentext.net/) A Canadian indexer, OpenText presents a tightly structured search specification format for exploring within URLs, Web site summaries, titles of articles, or first level sub-headings, joining words or phrases with Boolean operators.

Savvy Search (http://eclecticwebs.com/coolsite/searcheng/savvy.html) Put this first in your list of search tools because of its simplicity and efficiency. It's another one of those piratical systems that lets true search engines do most of the work, then displays the results. Although it identifies the sources of what it has found, it removes the ads from the pages before displaying them. If it seems to you that there is something un-

N   NETSCAPE NET SEARCH

LYC S
Get Lycos
or get lost

| Yellow Pages | RoadMaps | TOP 5% | PeopleFind |
| Classifieds | CompaniesOnline | City Guide | StockFind |

Go Get It

NEWS	SPORTS	MONEY
TRAVEL	TECHNOLOGY	HEALTH
SCIENCE	EDUCATION	LIFESTYLE
CULTURE	SHOPPING	KIDS
BUSINESS	ENTERTAINMENT	CAREERS
FASHION	GOVERNMENT	AUTOS

France   Germany
U.K.   Sweden

LYCOS PRO™
WITH JAVA
POWER PANEL™
NEW! Click here

WHERE'S THE BALL?
CLICK ON YOUR GUESS

Try one of these additional search services:

LookSmart
WebCrawler
AOL NetFind
CNET
 SEARCH.COM
HOTBOT

Customize this page! Select your favorite search service to open automatically here.

Need help? More information is available.

MORE SEARCH SERVICES

The following search services use different methods to help you find what you're looking for. Check them out.

SEARCH ENGINES	WEB GUIDES	WHITE & YELLOW PAGES	TOPIC SPECIFIC	TIPS
AltaVista	Excite	Bigfoot	100hot Web Sites	
AOL NetFind	Infoseek	Four11	AutoWeb Interactive	
Electric Library	LookSmart	GTE SuperPages	Health InfoNet	
HOTBOT	Lycos	ON'VILLAGE	RENT.NET:	
WebCrawler	CNET SEARCH.COM	Yellow Pages	Apartment Search	
	Yahoo!	WhoWhere?	Thomas Register	
		World Pages	of American Mfrs.	

| Guide to Internet ▼ | go | | International Search ▼ | go |

If this feature does not seem to be working, you should download the JavaScript Enabled Netscape Navigator.

| NETSCAPE HOME | DOWNLOAD SOFTWARE | CUSTOMER SERVICE | TECHNICAL SUPPORT | SEARCH & CONTENTS | WEB SITE ADVERTISING |

Corporate Sales: 415/937-2555; Personal Sales: 415/937-3777; Government Sales: 415/937-3678
If you have any questions, please visit Customer Service, or contact your nearest sales office.

This site powered by Netscape SuiteSpot servers.

FIGURE 5-3   *Lycos Home Page*-(Lycos Inc.)

fair about that, not far removed from copying software, up to now no one has contested the practice.

WebCrawler (http://www.webcrawler.com) Acquired from the University of Washington in mid-1995 by AOL, Web-Crawler is another spider with commercial aspirations.

Yahoo! (http://www.yahoo.com) Don't be put off by the title, an acronym for Yet Another Hierarchically Officious Oracle. Originated by two Stanford University students who took it out of academe into the commercial world with hardware and network resources provided by Netscape Communications, it is perhaps the most popular site among cyber-surfers. Yahoo! has assembled a broad collection of subjects, both entertaining and erudite, and remains open to additions. Contributions are moderated, resulting in little that is frivolous and contains surprising depth in many topics. Articles are analyzed and ranked for popularity. Review it regularly and you can always see what's new, what's "cool" and what's popular. Yahoo! was one of the first search services to commercialize as businesses saw the potential in putting banners before thousands of people daily.

U.S. Federal Government Sources These are not subject trees, but together they make up an enormous direct source of information. The Library of Congress Web site carries descriptions and commentary of its major exhibits over the past several years, access to its online catalog and indexes to other WWW services. These lead to the Department of Transportation and NASA Web pages. Separately, the Smithsonian Institution has put its OPAC, Smithsonian Institution Research Information System (SIRIS), up as a Web site. I defy any dedicated bird-watcher to build a more comprehensive biblio-

N | NETSCAPE NET SEARCH

Search

My Yahoo! - Today's News - Stock Quotes - Classifieds - Personals - Chat

Arts	Employment	Health	Media	Reference	Software
Business	Entertainment	Internet	Movies	Regional	Sports
Computers	Games	Investing	Music	Science	Travel
Education	Government	Kids	Recreation	Society	Weather

Yellow Pages - People Search - City Maps -- More Yahoos

Canada - France - Germany - Japan - UK -- Chicago - DC - LA - NY - SF -- **Get Local**

Try one of these additional search services:

LookSmart
WebCrawler
AOL NetFind
CNET
_SEARCH.COM
HOTBOT

Customize this page! Select your favorite search service to open automatically here.

Need help? More information is available.

Click Here!

MORE SEARCH SERVICES

The following search services use different methods to help you find what you're looking for. Check them out.

SEARCH ENGINES	WEB GUIDES	WHITE & YELLOW PAGES	TOPIC SPECIFIC	TIPS
AltaVista	Excite	Bigfoot	100hot Web Sites	
AOL NetFind	Infoseek	Four11	AutoWeb Interactive	
Electric Library	LookSmart	GTE SuperPages	Health InfoNet	
HOTBOT	Lycos	ON'VILLAGE	RENT.NET:	
WebCrawler	CNET SEARCH.COM	_Yellow Pages	_Apartment Search	
	Yahoo!	WhoWhere?	Thomas Register	
		World Pages	_of American Mfrs.	

Guide to Internet ▼ go   International Search ▼ go

If this feature does not seem to be working, you should download the JavaScript Enabled Netscape Navigator.

| NETSCAPE HOME | DOWNLOAD SOFTWARE | CUSTOMER SERVICE | TECHNICAL SUPPORT | SEARCH & CONTENTS | WEB SITE ADVERTISING |

Corporate Sales: 415/937-2555; Personal Sales: 415/937-3777; Government Sales: 415/937-3678
If you have any questions, please visit Customer Service, or contact your nearest sales office.

Copyright © 1997 Netscape Communications Corporation

This site powered by Netscape SuiteSpot servers.

FIGURE 5-4   *Yahoo! Home Page* (Yahoo! Inc.)

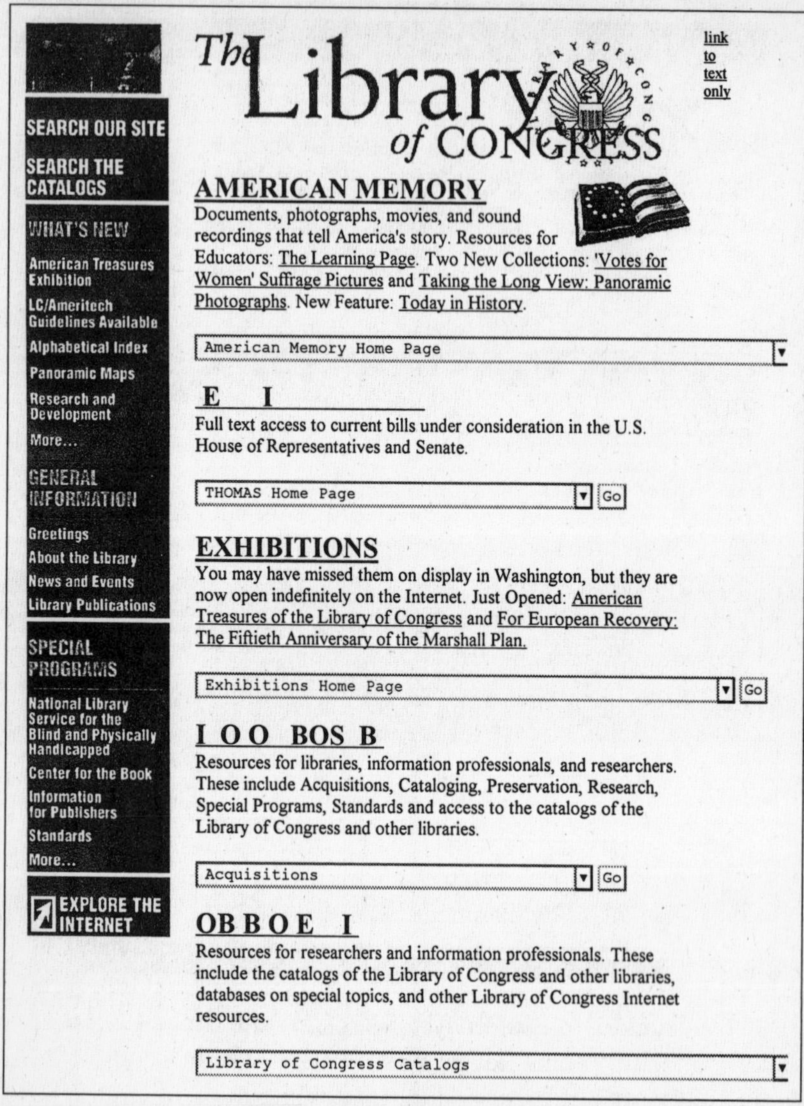

link to text only

The Library of Congress

AMERICAN MEMORY

Documents, photographs, movies, and sound recordings that tell America's story. Resources for Educators: <u>The Learning Page</u>. Two New Collections: <u>'Votes for Women' Suffrage Pictures</u> and <u>Taking the Long View: Panoramic Photographs</u>. New Feature: <u>Today in History</u>.

| American Memory Home Page | ▼ |

E I

Full text access to current bills under consideration in the U.S. House of Representatives and Senate.

| THOMAS Home Page | ▼ | Go |

EXHIBITIONS

You may have missed them on display in Washington, but they are now open indefinitely on the Internet. Just Opened: <u>American Treasures of the Library of Congress</u> and <u>For European Recovery: The Fiftieth Anniversary of the Marshall Plan.</u>

| Exhibitions Home Page | ▼ | Go |

I O O BOS B

Resources for libraries, information professionals, and researchers. These include Acquisitions, Cataloging, Preservation, Research, Special Programs, Standards and access to the catalogs of the Library of Congress and other libraries.

| Acquisitions | ▼ | Go |

OB B O E I

Resources for researchers and information professionals. These include the catalogs of the Library of Congress and other libraries, databases on special topics, and other Library of Congress Internet resources.

| Library of Congress Catalogs | ▼ |

Navigation sidebar

SEARCH OUR SITE

SEARCH THE CATALOGS

WHAT'S NEW

American Treasures Exhibition
LC/Ameritech Guidelines Available
Alphabetical Index
Panoramic Maps
Research and Development
More...

GENERAL INFORMATION

Greetings
About the Library
News and Events
Library Publications

SPECIAL PROGRAMS

National Library Service for the Blind and Physically Handicapped
Center for the Book
Information for Publishers
Standards
More...

EXPLORE THE INTERNET

FIGURE 5-5 *Library of Congress Home Page* (United States Government)

graphy on birds than what SIRIS makes available. The once-secretive Central Intelligence Agency's Web site, includes the *CIA World Fact Book*, a superb collection of recent, detailed information about every nation in the world, with maps. This is probably the best source you could find for current geographical and political information. Several other government sites are listed in the Appendix.

Reference Sites

Amazon.com Books Still feel books are better? Live miles from a good bookstore and prefer to purchase by mail? Go to http://www.amazon.com, where they take an upbeat approach to book retailing. The Seattle company claims it offers more book titles than any of the major chains. Recent *New York Times* book reviews, full ISBN/LC descriptions, even author interviews and e-mail addresses are available online. Everything is discounted (add shipping costs), and a projected availability is given for each book. This serves as a splendid supplement to *Books in Print*.

Not to be outdone, Barnes and Noble also has an online bookstore.

Britannica Online (http://partner.netscape.com/comprod/business_solutions/commerce/customer/encbri.html) This is *The Encyclopaedia Britannica* on the World Wide Web, by paid subscription. For serious researchers who make regular and extended use of encyclopedias, it might well be worth the money. Various levels of service are offered, and a free trial is available. Cross-referencing and speed in accessing the content of the full publication improves on frequent trips to the library. You save on carfare and the time it takes to flip the pages.

Deja News (http://www.dejanews.com)   For the best way to find newsgroups of interest (see Newsgroup Housekeeping, earlier in this chapter), consider this to be the OPAC of Usenet newsgroups. You provide the key words and Deja News applies WAIS techniques within Usenet to give you a list of articles and associated newsgroups. It is fast and remarkably thorough, even exploring months-old archives. See also UseNet FAQs.

New York Public Library (http://www.nypl.org)   Go beyond the NYPL's WWW home page, a typical introductory list of library resources, and look into the catalogs. Use telnet to browse CATNYP, the Research Libraries catalog, or LEO, the branch libraries catalog. NYPL card holders can also use LEO to examine periodical and newspaper indexes.

New York Times (http://www.nytimes.com/)   A WWW condensation of the news sections of the familiar daily, it includes CyberTimes with current newsworthy articles on Internet, computers, and software. A sub-heading, "Navigator," provides an up-to-date guide to Internet sources.

UseNet FAQs (http://www.cis.ohio-state.edu/hypertext/faq/usenet/FAQ-List.html)   Ohio State University maintains MIT's archives of frequently asked questions in Web format. Searching for desired FAQs through a browser gets you to the desired text a good deal easier than by FTP. This supplements Deja News.

There are hundreds of other jumping-off places catering to many interests, several linked to popular subject trees. Work from the trees listed above (more in Appendix A), and a companion volume such as *The World Wide Web Unleashed, The*

Internet Yellow Pages, or *The New York Times—CyberTimes—Navigator.* Newsgroup references and periodic explorations will reveal new discoveries almost daily.

The Edge of the Web

Home pages are pointers to information sources, not detailed indexes of articles. Rarely will you find a precis. Nor is there is a discernable pattern to the selection of entries in home pages. They are essentially lists of what the compilers thought would be of wide interest. One must be persistent in searching, and patient with what is found or unfound. Searches can be fast or fulsome, with results that are fancy or frustrating. You will need to scan each article to learn its worth to your own projects.

You know you are at the edge of the Web when you are looking at a document without hypertext. The same applies to a Gopher search, even one that yields nothing.[6] You can go no further in the same direction, and it is necessary to back up and try elsewhere. Theoretically, the edge is where the information lies, in server files of plain text, tables, perhaps with informative graphics. All that preceded it was research work. Like taking a book down from the library shelf or printing out pages from a journal, you have arrived at the source.

Internet Resources: An Assessment

The ultimate value of the Internet is a matter of some controversy. Material found on the Net is unlikely to have the broad scope of that found on similar subjects in many libraries. WWW often leads enticingly to pages that are little more than advertisements for coming attractions (often stated as "under construction") or pointers to the physical locations (libraries and museums) of actual documents. Subject matter collections are chiefly the result of recent, user-specified submissions. Compare this with the long periods of collection development by professional librarians. Currently the physical nature of the Internet limits the presentation and depth of any subject: bandwidth restricts the usefulness of graphics and storage and file transfer considerations inhibit extensive text coverage; annotation and citation practices lack the control imposed by book publishers; references within useful material are sadly lacking or have been severely abridged; articles are not subjected to the rigorous peer review required of academic research; authors, newsgroups, and Web site maintainers are often students who move on, sometimes without replacement. Browser presentation of html is standard, but there is little in the way of style precepts for document content—nothing equivalent to *The Chicago Manual of Style*, although efforts are being made to achieve something equivalent to that.

Internet files delivered through mailing lists and searches do have characteristics that set them apart. Speed of access is foremost. Most OPACs are open to telnet connection, and a reliable bibliography based upon multiple catalog searches can be assembled in less time than it would take most people to travel to their local library. Newsgroup topics are often far ahead of libraries since it takes only an e-mail message to post new information, and Web sites point to hundreds of collections of introductory and descriptive material that would otherwise require multiple exchanges of letters or phone calls to collect. Museums' Web pages typically contain the full wording of descriptive panels and brochures making up their exhibits.

Perhaps the most subtle quality of Internet information is its modernity. As academe and the government change with the times, so does the Internet. Newsgroups tend to focus on contemporary topics, reflecting what is of current interest on university campuses—computers, sociology, pop music, films, as well as topics many would consider offensive. Discussions on last week's world happenings and statistics on current issues abound. To follow the arts, computers, sports, or high technology, the Internet is the first instead of the last place to look. It is also appealing that information content is certain to evolve along with the applications that deliver it. That alone warrants continued attention.

6

The Human Element

When you feel you have exhausted the electronic pathways, or if you just feel exhausted by your travels, it's time to collect information from real people, by phone and face to face. Electronics helps with efficient techniques for accomplishing both. There's more to it than just talking.

Telephone Inquiries

During library and online research you might discover information sources that are reachable by telephone. In chapter 2 you learned about the Federal Information Center, and *The Yearbook of Experts, Authorities and Spokespersons* was cited, listing hundreds of sources. Still others may be found on the Internet. Even the reference desk of your local library can be a valuable telephone resource. Often "telephone tag" interferes with the efficient retrieval of information. Call-back no-

RecNo	19	Date	7-24-95		Time	10.15

Query | Wording/facsimile of 18th century merchant marine shipping papers?

Source Smithsonian Maritime   **Phone** 1-201-234-5678

Responder Paulson, John   **Referred** ☐

Action Checking on microfilm photos; will call.

RespDue 7   **Completed** ☐

FIGURE 6-1   *A Telephone Inquiry Database Record*

tations on a sticky pad may suffice for one or two such calls.

Unfortunately, the strangers you call can easily forget you. You might even forget or confuse the names of your target contacts. When a stranger whom you've phoned calls back, are you ready to recognize the person at once? Here's how the power of the computer next to the telephone can overcome the follow-up problem.

Figure 6-1 shows a suggested format for an inquiry record that you should keep in a simple database program. It serves much the same purpose as sticky notes, with the added element of building an organized history. Some people use personal information managers (PIMs) for this. Keep the program or PIM active as you pick up the phone, and review it for follow-up reminders. When in contact with an apparently forgetful source, a courteous reference by time or date to prior calls and promises will often hasten completion of your request. Strangers dealing with strangers is more the root of follow-up failure than is willful obstruction. Remember that people like to be asked about their jobs and their opinions in their areas of expertise. Make a friend of the person at the other end, and the information will flow.

Interviewing Tactics

You can add human interest to your work by stepping away from the computer and out of the library to meet people one-on-one. You have something to write about, and they have something to say. Interviewing gives you a refreshing change of pace. Many people with little knowledge about the information age have insights and memories that make up a rich lode of colorful commentary. Use these guidelines for effective interviewing techniques.

1. *Do your homework.* Before the actual meeting, complete most of your research on the subject matter and the person to be interviewed. Compile references to news articles, publications, notes for discussion, and a sequenced list of questions on 5″ × 8″ index cards. Leave space on the front of the card for the interviewee's address and phone number. Verify that data before starting the formal interview.

2. *Capture it live.* Use a suitable tape recorder. Know its capabilities: How directional is the mike? To what extent will it tolerate ambient noise? How much recording time remains before the tape runs out? Telephone recording is more difficult to accomplish, although attachments are available to do that with many types of recorders. In a number of states, it is illegal to tape a conversation on the telephone or in

person without informing the interviewee that this is being done. Most writers and reporters agree that it is proper ethics to let people know they are being recorded.

3. *Be fair.* Make sure the subject always knows when the recorder is on, especially if the interview is by telephone. A special I-am-recording signal is not necessary; just say so as you switch on or off. But avoid telephone interviewing if possible. You miss the nonverbal expressions and genial banter that make partners of you and your subject. There can even be an element of distrust that develops in phone conversations: Who knows what goes on unseen?

4. *Plan for the ultimate use of the tape.* Key the index numbers from the tape counter to notes you jot down on the index cards. Also use a note pad to supplement recorded conversation. Tuck the index cards inside the pad—they contain your interview script. Describe on the notepad the circumstances, environment as you observe it, appearances, gestures, or reactions not evident in the recording. While tapes are a good backup, learning to take good notes is best, as it can be onerous to go back through recorded interviews. Preserving notes and tapes can be a problem in legal cases. You may have good reasons for not wanting to show rough notes or a first draft to a lawyer or judge. Some writers say it is best to destroy everything.

5. *Dateline the conversation.* Open the tape with your own voice, stating the time, place, and name of the interviewee. Play that back in his/her presence to assess the recording quality.

6. *Work under agreeable rules.* Turn the recorder off, and set up guidelines for allotted time for the interview, usability of recorded words, off-the-record discussion, etc. Allow time in the interview for delays and diversions. Avoid breaks unless the conversation extends over an hour. Make sure there is agreement on all of this among all parties before you start. Although there is nothing to prevent the interviewee from changing the rules at any time, this simple introduction serves to put you both at ease. As the interview begins, let the person being interviewed be the timekeeper. If people are having fun, they'll go longer.

7. *Know what is quotable.* Maintain a clear understanding about attributing quotations: quotable by name, off-the-record, quotable but from a "confidential source," unrecorded, and for background only. The latter may or may not carry much weight, but sometimes helps to generate new leads or verify the veracity of other sources.

8. *Cooperation goes two ways.* The person being interviewed may want to review a typed script before anything is published. This can be cumbersome, and almost always should be avoided. Try to limit this kind of checking, if required, to factual content only, but it may be necessary to show a full typed transcript to achieve adequate cooperation. If the interview is to be reviewed in typescript, be sure to include every spoken word on the tape. Respect the person's right to strike out what is considered inappropriate.

9. *Sweeten the environment.* Put the person you're interviewing at ease with perhaps a compliment.

People are also flattered simply by being asked about their work, and will respond in kind.

10. *Stay interested.* Let the person being interviewed ramble. Avoid interrupting or hastening the conversation. Stay involved, perhaps merely by nodding or if the interview is by telephone, three useful conversational words are all you need: "Hmm," "Oh?" and "Really." The inflection on the last one can express agreement, incredulity, or nothing at all. While listening you can use a corner of your brain to compose the next portion of the discussion.

11. *Keep the discussion flowing.* Always be ready with the next question. The tape recorder does most of your listening for you. While the interviewee does most of the talking, you should never be at a loss for words or have to hesitate in preparation for the next question.

12. *Avoid promises.* Conform to the established ground rules and make no further commitments.

13. *Look for leads.* Ask for more sources as appropriate, not to imply the interviewee is inexpert on the subject matter, but to seek even more information.

14. *Defer the challenges.* Save the tough questions until the end. Bring them up almost as an afterthought, perhaps as you prepare to leave or hang up. In some circumstances, if you expect to be particularly provocative, put the tape recorder away, and pose the question with your final handshake. Remember the person's response, repeating it to yourself in silence, then ask the interviewee if it is okay to contact them again with additional questions if you find you need clarification or further information.

15. *Wrap up while alone.* When you can do so with-

out distraction write a loose narrative about the responses to any "testy" or unrecorded questions. Do this before listening to the taped interview. It is in effect your impression of the interview after the briefest lapse of time, as free of influence as you can be under the circumstances. Correlate the tape with notes taken during the interview. Use the index cards to record keys to the tape counter at various points and to your written notes. Preserve everything as you would other documents, and put a reference in your master list.

If you don't use a recorder, put your notes into formal writing as soon after the interview as possible. You'll have trouble deciphering your notes days or weeks later. Notes written soon after the fact are generally reliable transcripts.

Keeping Organized

Research projects have a way of taking on a life of their own. After you think you have collected all the information you need and are well into the writing phase, you are apt to discover new and useful information. You could be on the bus reading the morning paper when you come across an article containing something pertinent to your project. Clip it, write the date and source on it, and write down reference information. Sometimes it's as simple as seeing just the word you were searching for and couldn't conjure up a few days earlier. Here is where your pocket notebook or index cards come in handy amid everyday distractions. Write it down.

Creative people often sense a nearly continual stream of

consciousness concerning their work in process, as if their brain is operating on two channels. Their writing brain idles, whether they are balancing their accounts, painting a closet, or watching television. Then something occurs to them that could add to their written work, introduce an idea, or open up a new theme to be explored. That is when it's time to jot down as much as necessary to keep the idea percolating, and then take a few minutes to brainstorm. Write down any other ideas or thoughts that stem from the original word or thought that got your attention. Writers often continually take notes on subjects they might write about some day. It doesn't hurt either to keep a notepad by your bed: If you get a good idea at night you can write it down and check in the morning to see if it's worthwhile. If you don't write it down, it will probably slip away.

In the library, visiting museums, on interviews, recording the results of telephone inquiries, or exploring online databases, you will find yourself taking notes. To help identify the location of your search, purpose, and dates, label the top of a completed, numbered, and stapled set of pages with key words, pertinent to your outline or chapter topics. Or perhaps you use color-coded notepads as described in chapter 1. If you don't organize as you write, you will find yourself with a confusing collection of miscellaneous notes, bibliographic cards, tapes, photocopies, etc.

If you already have a jumble of notes and index cards, the best thing you can do in this confused state is to get down on the floor with the whole collection, and distribute each article, every individual paper, scratched note and recording tape into topical piles. Crawl around from topic to topic as you study, sort, label by category and finally assemble the collection in manila folders. Store these alphabetically, inserting cross-reference sheets into some folders when notes belong in multiple categories. I learned this invaluable idea from people who specialize in office efficiency.

Another thing you can do is to keep two folders (the kind with inside pockets) of unique colors that stand out among others. Label one "work in process" for papers you are currently handling that have been temporarily removed from their category folders. Reserve the other for all correspondence, sent and received (inquiries, thank-you letters, business matters), anything external to your creative work. These are the only two folders that you should allow out of storage. From time to time as you get wrapped up in your work you may violate your own rule. Nothing as mundane as filing should interfere with your creativity. That will get you disorganized again, so take the mess back down onto the floor. You'd be surprised at how this process helps you stay in control and crisps up your creative process.

Checkpoint

The critical portion of your research work is coming to a close. By now you should have a master list of bibliographic references, and periodical and journal extracts. The identities of online pages are either printed or captured in computer files, photocopies, and microfilm printouts, and index cards, notes, and transcripts of tape recordings from which you could extract direct quotations are in your folders. Remember that as you review entries in the master list, you should copy entries of books that you have used into the formal bibliography in the lower portion of that file, and edit the copied lines into proper bibliographic format. This master list is your investigative log and bible, and may contain additional notes for your own reference. The formal bibliography will eventually be separated from its parent to become a part of your finished work. Reorganize your collection of material once more, and take a deep breath. It's time to start writing.

7

Potholes, Obstacles, and Other Considerations

In putting the results of your research into manuscript form you move into a transition period. Take care here and you will have less concern when you deliver the completed work to an editor. There are cautions to be observed and dangers to be avoided. Careful attention to details can make an editor more of a partner in your project. The tips in this chapter will help you achieve that goal.

Private Papers

A fruitful source for nonfiction writers, not mentioned until now, is that of private collections—documents, artifacts, photographs, and letters, classified under the general heading of personal papers. The originators or owners need not be well-known people. The papers' value could lie in a combination of age and insight (Civil War correspondence for example), or diaries of common people associated with important events. I mention them here because they carry with them inherent risks.

There is only one way to work with another's personal papers, and that is with photocopies. Never handle the originals, except to evaluate them for use and perhaps to reproduce them, ideally in the presence of the owner. The owner of the papers should be encouraged to do the copying, so that what might be of great value never leaves that person's possession. You should bear the costs of copying and make yourself at least two copies. Retain one as a complete working set and hold onto another as backup. Then you can rearrange and staple pages, make marginal notes, and highlight important passages.

If it's difficult for the owner to provide copies, first establish an inventory, naming and describing each item with page quantity (noting whether single or double sided), being certain that you both agree on the final list. This tedious practice may be enough to convince the owner to find a way to pass copies directly to you. If originals must be delivered, register and insure them. Upon delivery, immediately return to the owner an inventory of received items. Later, when returning the goods, include a shipping copy matching that list. The period on loan should be short, and generally only for photocopying. These precautions help to avoid culpability in case of damage or loss. Imagine the result of your published work will be increased by a hundredfold by the inherent value of the papers you have worked with.

Delivery of copies implies the need for permission to use. If there is any doubt of this, write the owner a letter stating your intent. In some circumstances it might be wise to draw up a contractual agreement giving you the right to first-time use of the material. Note that the owner may not have the right to give permission to reprint or reproduce the item. For example, you may possess a letter of mine. You own the document. You can sell it, trade it, etc. But the copyright is mine and so no one can quote it in print without my permission. This rule also applies to letters and other unpublished material of people long dead; the heirs own the copyright.

When you are finished with the borrowed letters, it's advisable to send a letter of thanks. Also prepare a short paragraph for inclusion in the book recognizing the owner's contribution. More than courtesy, recognition specifies the source of your information, the names of those who helped you, and the implied legitimacy of their right to share that material.

Electronic Copies

Information delivered by diskette, file transfer, data capture or e-mail requires special consideration. Before exchanging files with someone else, make a trial run to avoid misunderstanding and prove compatibility. When two people discuss data exchange by diskette, are they talking about the same media formatted for the same computer architecture (mainframe, midrange workstation, Unix-based workstation, Macintosh, or IBM-compatible microcomputer), using the same code (binary or ascii)? Is the data compressed, and if so, does the recipient have a suitable decompression program? Are formatting codes included, and for what word processing program? Graphical information is most prone to usage differences between computer programs. The recipient must have the proper graphics-viewing program to read any of a dozen or so formats.

Beyond the basic issue of machine compatibility are those of ownership and permission for use. The next section discusses copyright precautions. Unless your information source is the federal government (even then under rare circumstances), you should assume the material is copyrighted. Books such as the Bible, many classics, and texts of long dead authors may be in the public domain, but don't assume they are. Your source could be a revision or translation made expressly for the medium. Review any material electronically received for identification of ownership. If missing, make the best effort you can to find the copyright owner. Make sure you record your own direct and indirect sources in obtaining permission. Then try to trace back to the origin. Use nothing directly that is not your own without attribution, and often without explicit permission. (See the section on Fair Use.)

Copyright Considerations

Words, proper names, symbols, and usually titles are not subject to copyright protection, but they may be trademarks identifying unique commercial products. The trademark symbol, ™, following a word, phrase, or logo says that its owner is claiming certain rights. It has been published and the originator may have applied for registration with the U.S. Patent and Trademark Office. After appropriate investigation, when registration is granted, the owner gets legal protection in using the symbol, and shows this with the ®. Trademarks, or their equivalent for services, service marks, generally present few problems. Care should be taken not to confuse ownership, to clarify intent. It may be appropriate to include a listing in the publication's front matter, stating proper ownership of each trade or service mark referenced and not to suggest that the owner has endorsed the writer's work.

Copyright registration is the responsibility of the Library of Congress Copyright Office, but registration is not a requirement for protection. Electronic media have the greatest potential for copyright violation, due as much to misunderstanding as to ease of reproduction. The laws themselves are not always clear, unable to keep up with advancements in technology. Electronic distribution presents the biggest threat to a writer's proper compensation, is the hardest to track, and confronts legislators with the most complex challenges.

Protection given under the 1976 Copyright Law was broadened in 1989 when the United States aligned its laws with all nations subscribing to the Berne Copyright Convention. Since then, nearly every product of intellectual effort, created and distributed by any means, is protected—music, art, computer programs, and text. The item need not carry the familiar copyright notice © formerly required under U.S. law. Thus anything you find in newsgroups, mailing lists, gopher or web sites, with or without a notice, should be assumed to be copyrighted—including, of course, personal e-mail. Copyright law is largely civil law. Violation is not apt to be a criminal act, but it does expose you and your publisher to potential lawsuit. In a litigious society, failure to conform is risky.

Fair Use

Meanwhile, fair use of material for a variety of purposes is more broadly defined in the United States than elsewhere, but note the distinction, alluded to above, between published and unpublished material. It is here that economic rights bump into the revered First Amendment. Valid use of excerpts is permissible for education, commentary, news reporting, even parody. A quote should be brief, attributed to the author, represent a relatively small portion of the original from which it came, and not affect the market for the work.

In these circumstances, it is generally not necessary to get permission for use, and no compensation is due.

Careful compilation of your master list with frequent reference to it as you write can keep your conscience clear. Thorough referential footnotes or endnotes keep editors happy. Annotation gets in the way of how-to texts and books meant for light reading. Keep notes anyway for your own use by marking up a draft copy in the margins. When your manuscript is complete, everything should have protective support by direct attribution within the text or by marginal pointers to references in your master list. Be wary that material from a computer database often differs from that of its source book, even when a service references the text of the book. If the electronic version of the database refers to the book, your attribution should be to both.

Rewrite longer quotes in your own words if you are doubtful about staying within fair use conventions. Many people plagiarize unconsciously or because they are unable to rewrite well enough. A traditional rule is to work from at least three sources; don't actually look at the open books as you write. Still, give credit to your sources. Do you give the reader the impression that what you have written is yours, or do you reference the originator? Paraphrasing someone's original thought could still be considered plagiarism if no credit is given.

Permission should always be sought for reproduction of graphical images, diagrams, or photographs. Here again, the electronic age presents more challenges than solutions. Is the home page of a WWW site a small portion of the original work? Typically it contains a graphic, and may be the originator's complete work.

The Permission Request

It is a simple task to seek permission. You might start the process with an e-mail request, but your goal should be to get the okay in writing. Publishers expect that. Produce a letter in the following form, and send it to the copyright owner with a self-addressed, stamped envelope.

To: (addressee)

This is a request for permission to reprint the following material from your publication. (Here describe the publication, title, author, date, page numbers from which extracted, etc.. Give full URL of Internet documents.)

The material is to appear (in its original state/with changes as noted below), in a book/article which (publisher's name) is currently preparing for publication. It is tentatively titled (your title), by (your name), approximately (quantity) pages, and due for publication (date) in a press run of (quantity) copies.

I am requesting nonexclusive world rights to use this material as part of my work for all editions.

Unless requested otherwise, acknowledgment of the source will be given in conventional publishing format. If you are the copyright holder, may I have permission to reprint the material as described? If you are not the copyright holder, or if additional permissions are required, please provide me with the appropriate information.

Duplicate copies of this letter and a self-addressed envelope are enclosed for your convenience. Please note any conditions or restrictions that apply.

_____   _____

Approved   Date

Keep a copy of the original mailing on which you should note the pertinent pages of your own manuscript to which it applies. When the approval is returned, copy it for submission to your publisher and clip the original to your annotated copy.

The High-Tech Disclaimer

Modern technology advances faster than the printed word can keep pace. New versions of software are released close to the time that textbooks on the prior releases are being printed. Rapid change is a reality today. The author must either be vague and elusive or risk inaccuracies due to unforeseen changes in the subject of the work. This disclaimer is often used:

> The information contained herein is provided as is with no express or implied warranties. While every effort has been made to ensure the accuracy of information, the author and/or publisher assume no responsibility for errors or omissions, or for damages resulting from the use of the information contained herein.

Copyright: The Other Side

Writers sometimes share their research or try out work in process via the Internet or other online facilities. In spite of earlier cautions about lawful protection of rights, you should consider that in these circumstances all practical copyright protection vanishes. Anybody could pick up your words and use them any way they want.

Why are you sharing your work? If you want validation of

facts, list them without wrapping them in your own style. If you want commentary on your style, distort or exclude the facts. To explore the level of interest, ask forthright questions about the topic. Take subsequent correspondence out of public view such as forums or newsgroups, using e-mail at first, in writing if interest continues. Finally, should it appear that one or two people could contribute by reading and commenting on your work, and you can't meet face-to-face, at least get a formal acknowledgment of the work in writing. Don't distribute annotated or polished drafts. Hold those for contractual performance. Often you will do better to let publishers find their own reviewers, as they are closer to the potential market.

The Work Log

Like keeping a master list of sources, you should also keep a computer-based log, listing by date the significant developments in your project. A history of sites visited would be helpful in case you need to backtrack. This might reference extended database inquiries with comments on success rate, lengthy connection time, and value to your project. The log should quantify the time you devote to each phase of your work. Summarize your expenses periodically. Identify by date any important correspondence, occasions of interviews, major milestones in your project, even your disappointments and joys. Gathering information and writing about what you have collected is demanding work.

8
Wrap-up:
The Writer's Toolkit

Like any craft, the task of seeking information requires working tools. Fortunately, most research tools are inexpensive. You probably already have much of what you would ordinarily need. The one exception is a personal computer furnished with data communications capability. Active writers usually have access to one for word processing, but I intend to take you further. Computer costs can be proportional to the extent and importance of your research, and by applying a few simple techniques, you can easily keep them in control.

Funds

Some writers give little thought to keeping a working fund, choosing instead to spend money out-of-pocket for development expenses. That may work for small projects or until cash gets tight, but it interferes with good research practices. You will need money for stationery items, postage, copying services, telephone, travel, and network connections. If you write for income, those are tax-deductible expenses. By taking a businesslike approach and planning for anticipated needs, you'll know how far your research efforts can go.

Take on no writing project without making a reasonable cost estimate for the proposed work. Since most of your expenses will probably arise from the gathering of information, it makes sense to budget for them. Faithfully take that approach and you'll be able to quote a fair and competitive fee for your writing effort.

A trade magazine editor once asked me to conduct a survey and produce an article on a new technical position being introduced in many companies. Hers was a national magazine, and she didn't want the article to have a regional slant. The offer seemed attractive, but to make it worth my while it appeared I would have to do all but local interviews by telephone instead of onsite. After some discussion, I allocated a fair portion of my fee for travel to get a feel for the working conditions of those being interviewed. When I explained that to the editor, I succeeded in negotiating a higher fee. Throughout the project I kept the working fund in mind.

The discipline enabled me to give the article a national flavor through one triangular economy flight, several evening phone calls, and a local meeting with a person traveling to my own city. Eighteen people are represented in the article, coming from a geographical cross section of the industry.

Your working fund doesn't have to be money in the bank. It can be based on anticipated advances or the accumulation of other usable resources. It could include a projected share of otherwise personal expenditures which you expect to apply to your writing revenues. Suppose, for instance, that you anticipate putting 2,000 miles on your car in pursuit of specific writing projects. At the rate of 31 cents per mile currently allowed by the IRS, $620 of funding will come from the monthly gas, oil and maintenance costs you will spend anyway. Although that is out-of-pocket funding, you impose control by advance identification of these research expenses.

There are other reasons to start with a planned working fund. You can use the simple statement, "my project is funded," to quell the curious and to open doors. When most professional writers mention a work in process they are apt to face the question, "Do you have a publisher?" Try responding with, "The project is funded," and let the questioners draw their own conclusions.

To get information about a warship in the opposite coast's mothball fleet, I felt a visit was necessary, not as a curious tourist, but in a professional capacity. I wanted to go much further into its innards than the main deck tour scheduled monthly for tourists. My planned book was then in the formative stage; no publisher was yet interested. I contacted the authorities with my request, explaining that my goal was a book, and "the project is funded." They realized that I wouldn't be willing to cross the country for a thirty-minute walk around. Not only did they give me permission to visit on my own schedule, but they arranged a three-hour guided tour. My funding amounted to an accumulation of frequent flyer points and a charge card for an overnight at a nearby Motel 6. The completed trip was key to getting a contract for the book's publication.

Of course you'll need some hard cash. A pocketful of quarters will be helpful in museums and libraries which require money for use of copiers and microfilm printers. If you travel while doing your research, use a credit card to keep work-related expenses separate. You'll get documentation of your major expenses regularly, and the annual fee could be a legitimate expense.

On the Internet you can find potential sources of grant money for writers, but it will take a diligent amount of research to produce a successful application. Any submission that meets grant specifications should include a well explained financial plan, based on a thorough understanding of the work necessary to produce the text. You must prove need, show the extent of your own investment of time and money, outline your financial and production plans, and state the objectives of your work. Your proposal will be more effective if based on records of earlier activities.

Financial Plan

A financial plan is a business worksheet. It is concerned with expenses, income, and projections of profit and loss during designated periods. This is particularly important for writers who may go weeks or months without revenue. They still will incur regular living expenses and costs in their professional operations. Even those who don't write for direct income, such as students and volunteers, should work under a financial plan. No matter how casually drawn up, it helps to focus efforts. Suppose a student in New Hampshire plans to write a paper on Martin Luther King Jr. In setting up a financial plan, the scholar would project travel to suitable libraries. It might become evident that the best sources of information are in Boston and Atlanta. Does the student have money for travel, or must inter-library loans be arranged? How will personal papers that are not allowed to leave the library be accessed? Inter-library loans, if available, will cost something for shipping, and possibly surety fees. Such circumstances might deter the writer from that particular subject and suggest that another subject would be appropriate, considering the writer's locale.

The professional writer should be rigorous in working up a financial plan for another reason. Authors are usually responsible for providing all materials used in publishing their works. How many photographs or pieces of artwork are envisioned, and what are the sources? How much travel will be required to gather information, and by what means? What will it cost to copy and ship the manuscript for reviews? List as many items as you can think of, arranged by time. Make a plan within the phases of your project. Working out a projected expense sheet is important if you work with deadlines. The plan is primarily for you, but in some circumstances, as in subsidized ghost writing, you may want to share the outline with your publisher. The more thorough and professionally assembled your financial plan is, the better the chance of selling your work to a publisher. Make a practice of working up an individual plan for every writing project you undertake. After you have done two or three, you probably can estimate closely the costs and time of subsequent projects. It is a great help in selling your services.

Table 8-1 is an example of a plan for producing an article on prize-winning travel agents. It is illustrative, with less detail than the actual working plan on which it is based. A similar preliminary study was useful in establishing an agreeable fixed fee for the work. Publishers are interested only in expenses to be underwritten, expecting to see details, not rounded estimates. Plan for all likely expenses. Even what's illustrated here shows that the writer's costs will reach $2,900 before the requested manuscript is submitted for editing.

Project Control

Many writers work on more than one article or text at a time. A person may be authoring a book that will take two or three

Table 8-1 Sample Financial Plan

Item	Note	1st Qtr	2nd Qtr	3rd Qtr	4th Qtr	Total
Meetings	1	$ 200				$ 200
Materials	2				$ 100	$ 100
Miscellaneous	3				$ 350	$ 350
Office costs	4	$ 50		$ 160		$ 210
Online research	5	$ 35	$ 250	$ 185		$ 470
Postage, shipping		$ 15	$ 10		$ 20	$ 45
Printing draft ms.					$ 35	$ 35
Research, local		$ 150	$ 50			$ 200
Subcontractors	6				$ 300	$ 300
Telephone		$ 20	$ 20	$ 20	$ 30	$ 90
Travel	7				$ 900	$ 900
Totals		$ 470	$ 330	$ 365	$ 1,735	$ 2,900

Notes:

1. Luncheon, author as host, to arrange interviews at National Convention, September; four guests expected.
2. Two color maps with permission to publish.
3. Legal review.
4. Copying, binding 50 pages in four copies (publisher, attorney, principals).
5. Online service connection; monthly fees, local Internet node.
6. Photographer services at convention.
7. Attend convention, Columbus, OH, interviewing award winners.

years to complete, but concurrently produces magazine articles to help pay the rent. Treat each work as a separate project, with its own plans for financing and tracking of completed events. The financial plan shows projected costs to complete. A plan for completed events keeps your effort on target. It should apply to all research/writing projects, not just those with a deadline. With sound planning and regular follow-through, you'll avoid wasting time on writing projects for lack of funds or casual work habits.

You don't need anything sophisticated to keep in control—just a simple means of accounting for money budgeted and spent, and a corresponding things-to-do list. Assign every writing project an identification name or number for control of expenses and events. It helps to categorize your activities, but you don't need detail. I find that two categories, Marketing and Production, work just fine. Others may break Production further into Research and Writing. How you classify your activities has to do with your own working style. Don't get so complicated that you must carry reminders of which category identifications to use. I assign a four-digit ID number to each potential writing project that I will spend time or money on. The four digits show the year the project was initiated and its order in the number of projects for that year. The number is preceded by the letter M or P. Thus M9602 and P9602 identify the marketing and production efforts involved with the second project started in 1996.

Most accounting programs allow you to assign a class code to income and expense items. This is where you use the project number. Write it on every check and sales receipt and periodically review the records to see how well you are controlling your costs.

Marketing time and expense may not have much to do with research work, but the rest of your activity loses meaning unless you track it. Later you will want to project the costs of certain marketing efforts. Build an information base keeping your past experience in mind. Proposals and query letters belong in the marketing category. Even that involves research. Has similar work been done recently? What magazines regularly publish comparable articles, and in what length?

Perhaps 15 percent of your costs and an equivalent amount of time will be devoted to this. To find a publisher for my first book without using an agent, I spent some five weeks writing and rewriting a proposal and assembling query letters. Then to reach the stage of a signed contract, I spent another week or two and some significant legal fees. These recorded business costs now serve as guides for subsequent activity.

List things-to-do as individual start- or completion-events, assigning tentative dates to each. The task "Write Chapter 7" is too vague for good control. That's not an event. Tasks are what occur between events. "Chapter 7 completed" is a clearly identifiable event. It identifies the end of a task. Apply your best estimate of time in calendar days to complete each task, allowing for delays. Often it helps to assign a priority to completion-events. Use digits, 1 being top priority, 9 being lowest, instead of high-medium-low, particularly if your list will be information for a computer program. Then you can sort events by priority with ease. Some tasks may overlap, while some are dependent upon the completion of others. Engineers define their projects by using network diagrams that reflect sequential and parallel tasks, so-called PERT charts, for project evaluation and review technique. Writers don't take on anything as complex as engineering activity, but this diagramming method helps to organize time. Plan your work, and you can make fewer trips to your sources.

Office Equipment

The most important research materials are the most common. It seems elementary to mention them, but they are necessary.

Before setting out on your project be sure you have stocked your office with:

- index cards, 3″ × 5″ and/or 5″ × 8″, whichever your preference; 5″ × 8″ is more versatile, but you could use both or either
- manila folders and a packet of replaceable folder labels; the specific contents of folders often seem to evolve into different species, and that's when you need to re-label them
- cardboard storage box(es), one for every major project
- notepads—multiple types in size, color, lined or cross-hatched, your preference
- stapler, manuscript binder clips, paper clips
- pencils and pens in multiple colors
- First Class 9″ × 12″ mailing envelopes, some padded
- inexpensive postal scale
- pocket-sized notepad with refills
- bound journal-type notebook with numbered pages
- business cards and stationery, your preference on style, bearing every means by which you can be contacted—voice, fax, e-mail, business and home addresses
- copier/printer paper, 20 lb.
- Rolodex, or address book

Your telephone can be one of your most direct sources of information. Include in your plans a reasonable amount of money for long distance calls. As you review the sources in this book (see Appendix A) and add entries to your address file, make notes about potential calling costs.

Hardware

Non-expendable items, generally costing over $50 and usable on multiple projects, fall in the category of capital equipment or overhead. If writing expenses are acceptable to the IRS as deductible against revenue, you may apply as much as $11,000 per year in direct cost for desktop computing equipment without doing cumbersome depreciation accounting. You shouldn't need one third that amount, even if you are completely upgrading your computer system. Good desktop computing equipment can be purchased for less than $2,000. This includes at least a 32-bit processor, color display, memory of 12 megabytes (MB, a million characters), hard disk of 2 gigabytes (GB, a billion characters), CD-ROM drive, 28,800-bits per second (bps) fax modem and all the necessary cables. That's a pretty extensive list of specifications. You could do with less, but more is better when it comes to computers. Allow funding also for online services, discussed fully in chapter 3.

My purpose is not to make specific recommendations on the computing equipment a researcher should have. If you can accomplish the essentials of word processing, some file management (names and addresses, book lists, etc.), and can handle data and fax communications, it matters little what company produced the hardware and the programs that run on it. Apple Macintosh or IBM-compatible hardware; MS-DOS, Windows, or OS/2 operating system—make those decisions with both guidance by computer experts and study on your part. Some schools and small publishers lean toward Macintosh because it is easy to learn and use. IBM-compatible equipment is more widely distributed, and perhaps more versatile. A wider selection of useful applications and more technical support is available for IBM-compatibles.

These days you can have the best of both worlds as Apple and IBM are moving toward compatibility with the advent of the Power Mac, which runs PC Windows.

If your machine is not connected to a local area network (LAN) you will need the modem for connection to a voice-grade telephone line (you need to disable your call waiting, *70, if your modem and voice line are the same). Color displays or monitors, once a luxury, are essential for graphical presentation, and a black and white ink-jet printer is more economical than a laser printer. It's nearly as versatile, but a bit more cumbersome in use.

CD-ROM drives have become essential components of computer hardware. While CD-ROMs are still an option, more and more software, graphic programs, and reference materials are being sold on compact disk. Library collections of CD-ROM disks for popular reference are in their infancy. Their potential becomes clear when you realize that a single disk has a capacity of 680 megabytes of data. That equals about 150,000 pages of printed text, or ninety minutes of full orchestra sound, or hundreds of images and video clips in combination with text. CD-ROM disks usually contain their own programs to extract and present the data they carry.

Be sure that the CD-ROM is MPC- (multimedia personal computer) compliant, meeting level 2 specifications. This means that the device supports delivery of sound and color graphics to your workstation. Again, seek the advice of a computer expert. Today's luxuries are destined to become tomorrow's standards.

You will also need to consider a backup tape system. This has more to do with a well-equipped office than with tools for research. As your collection of information grows, you need to consider the risk of loss. No matter how much care you exercise, if you work on a computer the risks of fire, flood, and the foibles of fools are high. Two or three hundred dollars invested in a tape drive, its backup/restore program, and a set of blank tapes could be critical. The chances of a crash, a virus, or an accidental deletion could be disastrous without a backup. Meanwhile, follow the user's guide that comes with your computer and copy essential material to diskettes.

Software

First, identify programs that are immediately important to you and your research. Don't buy what you don't need right away. When you do need it, a newer version will more than likely be available. Keep your shopping list short, taking the time to learn how to use each program before installing the next on your list. Review the computer trade magazines stocked in your public library and look for descriptions and mail order prices, commonly listed in small print on full-page ads. Don't order a thing until someone with expertise reviews your list for compatibility. To guide you, I'll start with items that writers I know have found useful.

Whatever computer you use, it needs an operating system. Many new computers come with one preinstalled. This almost unseen software converts your intelligent input through keyboard or telephone line to magnetically encoded data, screen displays, or printed output. It also supports the installed application programs. For modern writers, the computer application that is needed besides word processing is data communications.

Most operating systems support multitasking—the ability to do multiple activities simultaneously. That was once a high-tech luxury, which became a costly but common facility for the advanced user. Now it is a standard. Without it, you must stop the current application, for example, word processing, if you want to use a communications program to search an online card catalog, or look up a telephone number in a database. Multitasking simplifies switching and expands user capability. For instance, while I am composing this text with WordPerfect, my computer is receiving a fax of an article I requested just minutes ago from an online database. It prints with no action on my part. Text entry, interactive inquiry, fax receipt, and printing are taking place concurrently. Multitasking can make a busy person even more productive!

A word about programs. Many writers use WordPerfect or Word. Publishers will almost always accept manuscripts delivered on diskette or by modem in these formats. When you submit your manuscript, *always* include a hard copy of what's on the disk. Any word processor on the market these days will enable you to do the basic functions of editing, block copying and deleting, spell-checking and word-finding with an associated thesaurus, mail merge (combining form letters with lists of names and addresses) and routine file maintenance. Grammar checking programs are also helpful and are often included.

I've said it before and I'll say it again: A communications program is second in importance to a word processor. This is properly called a terminal emulator, meaning it makes a modem-equipped computer act as if it is directly connected to another computer. Use of a terminal emulator on a regular dial-up voice telephone line or a LAN-connected terminal opens up a world of useful information for the researcher. In addition to government and public library electronic catalogs, many colleges, universities, and associated institutions have online public access catalogs (OPACs) that can be accessed by anyone with a computer and a modem. You have seen, in chapter 5, how to tap into many of those.

The simple exchange of mail and small text files does not require modem speeds any higher than 9,600 bits per second, which is the minimum rated speed for transfer of fax files. Speeds of 28,800 bits per second (expressed as 28.8 kbps) are becoming standard for the more demanding transfer of large files—graphical images, programs, lengthy reports, etc. Coming along, but overkill for now, is 56K bps. Terminal emulators should support transfer of fax files residing within the computer. The modem recognizes the difference between fax and data transmissions, and the communications program converts fax data streams to readable characters. Text files can be sent or received; graphical images can be received, displayed and printed, but a scanner is necessary for sending images on paper. Some writers use scanners to scan key passages from their research into their laptops instead of taking notes by hand.

In shopping for communications programs, look for those that support fax modems. Four popular programs that serve the same purpose are:

- 3 Com
- Crosstalk
- Procomm Plus
- QuickLink

QuickLink is bundled with many newer fax modems, and has adequate function for text, fax transfers, and other modems. Your operating system may include fax and terminal functions, and possibly the ability to connect with one of the more popular commercial online database services.

After you get familiar with the process of dialing other computer stations for the exchange of information, you shouldn't be without another type of program called a "navigator," explained in chapter 5. Navigators are directly tied to online database servers or Internet access programs. They help the nontechnical user explore some very complex territory by replacing often arcane command language with selection menus. Their communications-handling functions are dedicated to interaction with a specific commercial service or through Internet service providers (ISPs). ISPs usually recommend suitable navigators for use with their facilities. Netscape is probably the most popular Web navigator. Windows 95 includes Internet Explorer, and OS/2 Warp provides WebExplorer with its Internet connection.

The next thing we need to discuss is spreadsheets. There are three well-known and very powerful spreadsheet programs:

- Lotus 1-2-3
- Microsoft Excel
- Quattro Pro

They include much more function than most writers require and costs are medium to expensive. Don't overlook shareware programs that can be found in the libraries of local bulletin board systems or those maintained by commercial online services. You only need something that allows row and column calculations, sorting of lists, and formatting and printing of data. You would use a spreadsheet to compile small databases (bibliographies, telephone numbers, names and addresses, etc.).

An accounting program is almost essential to keep good financial records. Quicken enables you to keep separate records for business and personal use, even for investments. Its ease of use has made it the most popular of all bookkeeping programs. Quickbooks is a version for small businesses, and as with Quicken, may come already installed with some new computers.

Database programs are expensive, offering far more function than most people need. People who do specialized data research will be familiar with the intricacies of the database program that aids their work. For them it is probably their prime application. Most of us can manage limited data manipulation with a word processor, spreadsheet, or an operating system utility.

Lately there's been a lot of talk on personal information managers, which have been highly touted. They are essentially automated things-to-do lists or schedulers. Again, you may find that your operating system gives you one among its utilities. If not, consider using a pad of paper. That has worked just as well for most people for centuries.

For some writers, graphics programs for the production of diagrams, charts, and drawings, while large, complex, and costly, could be essential. These are not, strictly speaking, researcher's tools. Graphics may enhance a writer's work, but if you are not versatile with anything more than a word processor at this point, move slowly, taking on these additional programs one at a time, and only as needed.

Another option may be to invest in Microsoft Office or Claris Works, with a collection of word processing, spreadsheets, and other programs. They supply all these functions and more, and again, often may come already installed with your new computer.

Voice Recorder

Even if you do not interview, a voice recorder is practical in much research work. A battery-powered hand-held device with a built-in microphone is best. They are inexpensive and can be found in most electronic retail stores, including the batteries and tapes. Some have dual speeds to reduce tape usage during long conversations. That helps later when searching for particular passages. Some recorders are sound-controlled so that they stop recording if no sound is registered and resume automatically as needed so tape isn't wasted during long pauses. Look for a recorder with a counter to help you index specific sections. Before making the final purchase, arrange to test the device with a fair amount of ambient noise. If that is satisfactory, it will make on-the-spot interviewing easier. Battery-powered recorders also come with power supplies to plug into a wall socket to conserve batteries. Some are equipped with earphones and foot-controlled on/off switches, none of which is costly if you choose to purchase them separately.

While a voice recorder is essential for good interviewing, it is also useful for note-taking. The major problem you might encounter is the embarrassment of being seen talking to yourself. Consider having to identify dozens of books as you walk through a library's reference stacks, note the specifics of a collection in a museum without tables and chairs, or observe and have to remember in detail, the exterior of a building or a street. You may find that recording these details using the voice recorder the best way to carry out these tasks. If you were to take conventional notes, the amount you'd need to write all the details may well leave your hand cramped and your notes virtually unreadable due to haste. It isn't much different from using your laptop.

9
A Look Ahead

Where will the electronic highway take us? Making predictions in the world of advanced technology is a hazardous exercise, but some future conditions are practically self-evident.

The stereotype of the typical electronic user is changing as we speak. Children in grade schools commonly use bulletin board systems. Some are even given assignments involving online searches. After all, the goal of the "information highway" is to make it as common as the daily paper. Ultimately, students will arrive on college campuses already accustomed to Internet access. The extraordinary publicity the Internet has received in recent years is drawing a wider cross section of the public into its domain. Introductory courses on computers and use of the Internet for senior citizens have become common in many communities. The three major online services even offer special rates and forums for members of the American Association of Retired Persons (AARP), and discussions on issues facing people over 50 are conducted regularly. The hope, of course, is that subscribers will make up a representative cross section of the population. That, in turn, could give rise to more polling activity and online opinion surveys on matters of wide interest.

An increase in educational courses from tutorials such as the University of Alabama's Roadmap by Patrick Crispen to completely electronic classrooms such as New York University's DIAL campus is a certainty. It takes a special skill to produce courses that make distant learning effective. The course developer must understand how the remote student thinks, anticipate questions, and explain concepts at just the right time. More than twenty years of development work in education via interactive TV has produced the know-how with little if any defrayment of costs. A broader use of the Internet will help defray any residual costs.

The once-sharp distinction between commercial online database services and the Internet, already starting to blur, will disappear. Subscribers must be given added value for their money—forums perhaps, unique content that is inaccessable elsewhere, and ease of use. Still, the risk of user frustration and early rejection of fee-based services continues. Standardization to users' satisfaction will be slow to develop. Competitive interests tend to stifle standardization, even as leading organizations strive to achieve it. Historically the government has tried to be a catalyst, but its record in the world of computers and telecommunications has not been spectacular. Online public access catalogs in libraries are ripe for simplified standards (one standard has already been defined), but there is little motivation for responsible owners and less funding to achieve the goal.

Regardless of what happens in the future, you can be sure that improvement in technology is guaranteed: ever increasing disk capacity, faster telephone lines, low-cost color printing will be the norm and not the exception. The possibility of a static RAM computer chip making disks of all types obsolete is already under study. Telecommunications improvements face vast changes under reduced government intervention and already announced competitive plans. Data transmission speeds will continue to increase within reasonable costs. Anyone about to buy a modem today would do well to invest something extra in higher speeds, comfortable that the investment will provide longer life before practical obsolescence.

As technology changes so will information sources and their supporters. Well over half the traffic on the Internet is commercial, sent to and from .com domains. Commercial on-line services will increase Internet offerings at reasonable prices, forcing Internet service providers to improve their services or drop out. Netscape, Microsoft, Prodigy, CompuServe, and America Online now offer graphical browser access to the World Wide Web at minimum-use cost, equivalent to that charged by most ISPs.

While Internet users resist commercial exploitation of the medium, marketeers see opportunity and are achieving success in getting their messages across. Internet users aren't buying much through the medium, however. They mostly trade information useful to their daily activity. The commercial "banners" (advertisements) flashed before them are no more troublesome than the ads on the sides of a bus or inserts in the folds of a magazine. It will take credit card security, soon to come, low pricing and/or sole-source availability to develop profitable Internet shopping centers. This should result in a segmentation of subnetworks. Clarinet, a commercial supplier of current-event newsgroups, is an example. Just as Usenet is delivered to ISPs for distribution, for a fee ISPs can subscribe to Clarinet's daily news, organized into the traditional categories of business, sports, arts, etc.

The cloudiest portion of my crystal ball concerns the use

of search engines. It costs money to maintain and operate these handy WWW sites. As the experimentation and development phases end, more and more of the operators take on advertising. Will the revenue achieved provide them adequate profit? Some include a hint in their introductory material that they may eventually charge a fee. This of course would reduce the number of regular callers and the attractiveness to advertisers. Will Web sites parallel the periodical publishing world, cluttered with costly ads and priced to the consumer for individual use and by annual subscription? It is not likely that cyber-surfers will be willing to pay regular fees to more than a few Web sites. How many magazine subscriptions do you take on before you tire of renewing what you hardly have time to read? Perhaps commercial exploitation will take on the format of cable TV carriers by bundling access to multiple sites together. (Is All 4 One a prototype of such practice?) Usefulness of search engines and value of their content will certainly influence their evolution. The Encyclopaedia Britannica, The American Library Association, and The National Endowment for the Humanities now guarantee rich query results within their individual purposes, a hopeful development.

Interchange of binary files is currently more in the nice-to-have category than essential-for-research. The problem lies in file storage and transmission bandwidth. Graphical files, of marginal use for the bandwidth consumed, will become worthwhile when technology and competition filter the frivolous from the functional. There is ample need for the latter—maps, architectural drawings, musical scores, photographs, all the substance of useful hardbound books.

Photographs and sound consume exponentially more computer capacity than does text. When most of us have access to more powerful computers, electronic resources will be as well illustrated (with accompanying sound) as printed books, take less space, and eventually cost less to buy. The downside of this is that, like television, there is commercial attraction in appealing to the public's lowest common denominator. We'll have to tread through a lot of trash.

More than anything else, CD-ROMs and online access affect the future role of libraries. At the New York Public Library, they have increased their print holdings while adding the wiring for hundreds of text-based terminals. As information compaction is reflected in CD-ROM disks, and broader content increases their reference value, libraries will make multiple CD-ROMs accessible by phone from library servers. Web-based updates to CD-ROM references will extend their life and utility. Microsoft's Encarta 98 (referenced in chapter 2) includes a yearbook builder for connecting to a dedicated Web site for monthly updates. Copyright concerns, destined to be addressed, are all that prevent making CD-ROMs available for borrowing. The first edition of a CD-ROM publication may cost thousands of dollars to produce but copies cost pennies. In a *New Yorker* article ("Byte Verse," February 20, 1995), Anthony Lane wrote of the four-disk package "The English-Poetry Full-Text Database" produced in England and containing the complete works of more than 2,200 poets starting in A.D. 600. (Price? Only $51,000.) That makes it a natural for access via telnet and FTP. Once sales cover the cost of production it could be offered at a reduced price and receive wider distribution.

Bibliophiles may shudder at such prospects. Take comfort that these changes will come slowly, amid controversy and at substantial overall cost. While printed books will retain their primacy far into the next century, the most effective writers will be those who keep abreast of the changes. This book, I hope, has shown you where they are happening and how to use the best of both worlds for your writing and research needs. We've covered a lot of territory since we stood together on the banks of the Charles River.[1] Keep traveling, and enjoy the trip.

Appendix A
Information Sources

Refer also to the Bibliography for CD-ROMs and Reference Manuals.

Internet Service Providers

Mecklermedia Corporation   Call 203-226-6967; e-mail to meckler@ junc.net; CompuServe, 70373,616. The easiest to research and most detailed source can be found on the Web at http://www. thelist.com, a directory service of Mecklermedia. Search by name, geographic location, area code—local, national, and international providers; specifics on services, prices, line speeds, etc.

Internet Navigators

Internet Explorer   Microsoft's browser for use with Windows 95. Download it without charge from http://www.microsoft.com/ to upgrade the early Windows 95 CD-ROM version.

NCSA Mosaic   WWW browser, no charge for single users. By FTP from ftp.ncsa,uiuc.edu. A site-licensed version of Enhanced NCSA

Mosaic for Windows is available from Spyglass, Inc.; call 630-505-1010; fax 630-505-4944; e-mail to info@spyglass.com.

Netscape Navigator Available at no charge, or comes pre-installed on hardware. Download from http://www.netscape.com., or by clicking on Netscape banners on several Web sites. For full details, call Netscape Communications Corp., 800-638-7483 or 415-528-3777; e-mail to info@netscape.com.

SlipKnot By FTP from ftp.netcom.com/pub/pbrooks/slipknot.

The Internet Adapter (TIA) Host and site license information from InterMind. For host, e-mail to tia-licensing@marketplace.com, or for single use, tia-single@marketplace.com; call 206-545-7803.

WebExplorer For IBM's OS/2 Web browser, call 800-342-6672.

WorldNet Service (AT&T) For Windows 3.1, Windows 95 or Macintosh, call 800-967-5363.

Internet Training Online

"Patrick Crispen's Roadmap for the Information Superhighway," a twenty-seven-lesson, online course (arbitrarily six weeks in length) available, without charge, from the University of Alabama. Receive lessons via e-mail or directly from the university's archives. E-mail to listserv@ualvm.ua.edu; leave subject line blank, and put get map package f=mail in the body of the message.

Or, aim gopher client to gopher://ualvm.ua.edu and select Network Resources, Services and Information. "Roadmap" has been distributed to several Web sites. Try http://www.brandonu.ca/~ennsnr/Resources/Roadmap/Welcome.html.

Online Sources
Academic Sources

Encyclopaedia Brittanica See World Wide Web section of this Appendix.

PROFNET Through CompuServe 73163,1362 or 76550,750;
e-mail to profnet@sunysb.edu.; fax to 516-632-6313.

See also listings under Voice Telephone Sources, and URLs listed
in World Wide Web section of this Appendix.

Commercial Online Services

America Online (AOL) For information 703-448-8700; to sign up
800-827-6364.

CompuServe Information Services (CSi) For information, call
800-848-8990; to sign up 800-848-8199.

Dow Jones News and Information Service For information or to
sign up, 609-452-1511.

Microsoft Network For information and to sign up, 800-386-5550.

Prodigy For information, 914-993-8000; to sign up, 800-776-
3449.

Federal Government Sources

Bureau of the Census http://www.census.gov/ Facts from the
last count.

Central Intelligence Agency The CIA World Fact Book is found
in a section of the Office of the Director of Central Intelligence
at http://www.odci.gov/cia; that, and much more that was once
secret.

FedWorld http//www.fedworld.gov/ Check this site first and do a
key word search through agencies of the Department of Commerce
for government data. Scientific, technical, and business-related titles
from NTIS, tax forms, and instructions from IRS—be the first
on your block to see them, and much more; http://www.fed
world.gov/ leads to telnet, gopher, and FTP facilities.

General Services Administration, including Federal Information
Center Start with http://www.gsa.gov/ and follow the menu
from there.

House of Representatives   http://www.house.gov/ It speaks for itself.

Library of Congress Introduction and general information is available by telnet from locis.gov. Telnet to marvel.loc.gov for the LOC catalog. Other U.S. government resources can be found at http://lcweb.loc.gov/homepage/lchp.html.

National Aeronatic and Space Administration http://www.nasa.gov/

National Archives Direct your gopher client to gopher://gopher.nara.gov, or WWW client to http://www.nara.gov. For information on available publications, e-mail to inquire@nara.gov.

National Institutes of Health   http.//www.nih.gov/

National Library of Medicine   http://www.nlm.nih.gov/

National Science Foundation   http://www.nsf.gov/

Smithsonian Institution For general information, call 202-357-1385; fax 202-633-9023; e-mail to siris@sivm.si.edu. Browse the catalog via telnet to siris.si.edu (port 23 may be needed); or terminal emulator connection to 202-357-4304, with modem at 1200 to 9600 bps, N-8-1. Web site is http://www.si.edu

Social Security Online   http:www.ssa.gov/SSA_Home.html. This site is sensitive to its users' interests and has everything one needs to know about the Social Security Administration, and can even provide a personal earnings and benefits statement.

Thomas   http://thomas.loc.gov/ Library of Congress legislative information, aptly named for Mr. Jefferson and always current as to status of bills. Thomas is popular with researchers and writers, and provides a link to the Library of Congress OPAC for additional information.

The White House   http://www.whitehouse.gov/ Less information comes out of this Web site than from the Oval Office, but it's popular with the voters.

Periodicals and Journals

UnCover Configure terminal emulation up to 9600 bps, N-8-1; dial 303-756-3600. Or telnet to database.carl.org. UnCover is also available through any CARL system library.

Pictures, Microfilm
Commercial Photographic Sources

Corbis Bettmann, 902 Broadway, 5th Floor, New York, NY 10010-6002. 212-777-6200; fax 212-533-4034; http://www.corbis.com /corbis. The famous Bettmann Archive is now owned by Microsoft's Bill Gates.

Library of Congress, Prints and Photographs Division, Washington, DC 20540. 202-707-6394; fax 202-707-6647; http://www.loc.gov/ rr/print/

Smithsonian Institution, Archives Center, Washington, DC 20560. 202-357-3270. http://www.si.edu/cgi-bin/image_archive.pl

Time-Life-Sports Illustrated. Time and Life Building, Rockefeller Center, New York, NY 10020. Time Pix Syndication, Room 25-05, 212-522-3866; Life Photo Service, Room 28-58, 212-522-4800; Sports Illustrated, Room 19-19, 212-522-2898; http://www. pathfinder.com

Wide World Photos, Inc., 50 Rockefeller Plaza, New York, NY 10020. 212-621-1930. Includes photo collection of the Associated Press.

Newspaper Reprints

University Microfilm Inc. Pageprint department. 800-521-0600. Full page reprints of back editions of major newspapers.

Publications

National Archives, College Park, MD. General reference information is available at 301-713-6800, Questions on records availability are handled at 202-501-5400 in Washington, D.C.

Regional Archives

New England Region, Waltham, MA   617-647-8100
Pittsfield Region, Pittsfield, MA   (geneology microfilm only) 413-445-6885
Northeast Region, New York, NY   212-337-1300
Mid-Atlantic Region, Philadelphia, PA   215-597-3000
Southeast Region, East Point, GA   404-763-7477
Great Lakes Region, Chicago, IL   773-581-7816
Central Plains Region, Kansas City, MO   816-926-6272
Southwest Region, Fort Worth, TX   817-334-5525
Rocky Mountain Region, Denver, CO   303-236-0817
Pacific Sierra Region, San Bruno, CA   415-876-9009
Pacific Northwest Region, Seattle, WA   206-526-6507
Alaska Region, Anchorage, AK   907-271-2441

Publications are available in the regional archives offices and in the National Archives Building in Washington, D.C. Ask for the catalogs of publications, posters, and facsimiles. For credit card orders for selected catalog items, call 800-788-6282, Monday through Friday, 8:00 A.M. to 4:30 P.M.

Many publications are available electronically through Fax-on-Demand at 301-713-6905. Note: you must call from a fax machine to order and receive documents.

Yearbook of Experts, Authorities and Spokespersons, An Encyclopedia of Sources   For information, call publisher at 202-333-4904.

Voice Telephone Sources

Federal Information Center, 800-688-9889, from 9:00 A.M. to 5:00 P.M., eastern time. WWW users should check out the Home Page http://www.info.gov/html

PROFNET, 800-776-3638.

WWW Subject Trees and Other Sources

See also Federal Government Sources.

Amazon.com Books   http://www.amazon.com This bookstore carries reviews from the *New York Times* and by everyday readers. Full bibliographic details and prices for a million books. No kidding.

The Librarian's Index to the Internet   http://www.sunsite.berkeley.edu/InternetIndex/ Is of much interest to librarians.

Britannica Online   http:/www.eb.com/ *The Encyclopaedia Britannica* on the Web. The full encyclopedia can be found at http://www.eb.com/ Businesses, schools (there is an academic version), and dedicated researchers might not be stopped by the cost.

Clearinghouse for Subject-Oriented Guides to the Internet URL http://www.clearinghouse.net/ University of Michigan's subject tree, takes users into gophers, ftp sites, guides to list servers, and newsgroups.

c/net inc   http://www.search.com Provides an efficient starting point to harness over 250 Usenet and WWW searches.

Deja News   http://www.dejanews.com/ A newsgroup search engine from Deja News Research Service.

EINet Galaxy http://www.einet.net/galaxy.html lets user set search perimeters within the alphabetical list of Galaxy topics, through Gopher sites, Web sites, or combinations of these. Among the Gopher sites threaded to EINet is Gopher Jewels, a list of about sixty information categories (subject trees).

Lycos   http://lycos.cs.cmu.edu/   and   http://www.lycos.com/ lycos-form.html. Free searching service, funded by advertising. Incorporates Point, which rates the top 5 percent WWW sites, and A2Z, reporting by category on the Web's most hyperlinked sites.

Netscape Sources The Internet White Pages lists domain names, e-mail addresses, and organizations in directories linked from http://home.netscape.com/home/internet-white-pages.html. It maintains a search page to other search engines such as Lycos at http://home.netscape.com/home/internet-search.html. User's browser must have Forms capability to submit search parameters.

UseNet FAQs URL http://www.cis.ohio-state.edu/hypertext/faq/ usenet/FAQ-List.html Uses http format of MIT's archives of frequently asked questions.

The Virtual Library http://www.infi.net/~cwt/index.html The first and perhaps only Web page classified by the Library of Congress and R. R. Bowker (LC 95-70795, ISBN 1-57000-044-1).

WebCrawler http://webcrawler.com Obviously another spider.

WWW Virtual Library http://www.w3.org/hypertext/Data Sources/bySubject/Overview.html Contains hypertext listings arranged alphabetically by topic. Its ancestor was CERN's original Web site.

Yahoo! http://www.yahoo.com/

Appendix B—Glossary of Terms and Acronyms

This list goes beyond the abbreviations and phrases used in the text, on the possibility that readers will want to explore both library and computer science further.

Refer also to Babel: A Glossary of Computer-Oriented Abbreviations and Acronyms at http://www.access.digex./net/~ikind/babel.html

ANSI	American National Standards Institute. Recommends standards for information processing.
AOL	America Online, commercial database service.
ARPA	Advanced Research Projects Agency. Originator of ARPANET, progenitor of the Internet.
ascii	American Standard Code for Information Interchange, a nearly universal method for representing readable text files in personal computers and across telephone lines.
AT&T	American Telephone and Telegraph Company.
baud	Bandwidth measure of the amount of data that can be delivered or received in a given period. Also a unit of signaling speed, at lower

	speeds equivalent to bits per second. Over 4800 baud, higher bandwidths are achieved by advanced electronic methods.
BBS	Bulletin board system
beta	Second letter of Greek alphabet, used as in "beta version" to indicate a program under test by the general public, prior to final version to be marketed.
BITNET	International academic and research network, connected to the Internet, and strong in the support of mailing list servers. *See also* CREN.
black box	An electronic device that accomplishes some task that few but its designers understand.
Boolean	Symbolic logic applied by George Boole to the laws of thought in the nineteenth century.
bps	Bits per second
BTW	E-mail short-speak for "by the way."
CARL	Colorado Alliance of Research Libraries. Also name of one of several OPAC systems.
CCITT	Comite Consultatif Internationale de Tele-graphique et Telephonique. A United Nations committee recommending worldwide communications standards.
CD-ROM	Compact disk—read only memory
CERN	Conseil Européenne pour la Récherche Nucleaires. The acronym continues, although the name has been changed from Conseil to Organisation. Laboratory for particle physics, and developer of the World Wide Web, based in Switzerland.
CIS	CompuServe Information System, commercial data base service; older terminology. *See also* CSi.
Client	User program for requesting services from a remote computer.
cpu	Central processing unit. The "chip" that is the heart of a computer.

CREN   Computer Research and Education Network, the name for the merger of BITNET and CSNET, q.v.

CSi   CompuServe Incorporated service mark.

CSNET   Computer Science Network. *See also* CREN.

CWIS   Campus-wide information system. Original venue for e-mail applications.

DD   Dewey Decimal classification number

DNS   Domain naming system. Hierarchical addressing scheme corresponding to network IP addresses. *See also* IP.

domain   Set of locally connected user and server stations.

DOS   Disk Operating System, developed by Microsoft; sometimes called MS-DOS.

e-mail   Electronic mail

emoticon   Used in e-mail to denote emotion, i.e.,:-) smiley face for joke, :-(frown for sadness.

FAQ   Frequently asked question

flame   Insulting or offensive correspondence

freenet   No-charge Internet connection, limited to e-mail and selected newsgroups, usually sponsored as an introductory public service.

FTP   File transfer protocol

FWIW   E-mail short-speak, "for what it's worth."

gateway   Computer connecting two networks with dissimilar protocols.

Gopher   (1) Navigator developed at the University of Minnesota to gather and distribute information; (2) client-server protocol for searching on the Internet.

GPO   Government Printing Office

GSA   General Services Administration

GUI   Graphical user interface displayed by the Macintosh, Windows or OS/2 operating systems, as opposed to a text-only display.

homepage   A web site's opening page (screen) associated with its URL.

home site   The Internet node to which a user's terminal is directly connected.

host	Computer to which terminals are connected for service. Can be local or remote, and has broader meaning than home site, q.v.
html	Hypertext markup language. *See* hypertext.
http	Hypertext transmission protocol. *See* hypertext.
hypertext	Character string, usually highlighted, linking to associated files or documents and identified with html, q.v.
id	Identifying descriptor; identifier
ILL	Inter-library loan
IMHO	E-mail short-speak, "in my humble opinion."
IP	Internet protocol for packet switching. IP addresses identify each network node.
ISBN	International Standard Book Number, developed by R. R. Bowker Company.
ISO	International Standards Organization, an agency of the United Nations
ISP	Internet service provider
ISSN	International Standard Serial Number
jewel	List of what someone has determined to be interesting gopher sites
k	Thousand (kilo)
kbps	Thousand bits per second
LAN	Local area network. Generally, cable-connected terminals, workstations, servers and hosts.
LC	Library of Congress classification number.
ListServ	Program for managing mailing lists. *See also* Majordomo. Used generically, "listserv" for a mailing list of subscribers focused on a particular topic.
LOCIS	Library of Congress Information System
Majordomo	Program supporting automated mailing list subscription service. *See also* ListServ.
MARC	Machine readable catalog. Standard format established by the Library of Congress.
MARVEL	Machine-Assisted Realization of the Virtual Electronic Library. The catalog of the Library of Congress.

mb	Megabytes (millions of bytes). Unit of measure for computer memory.
MPC	Multimedia personal computer, equipped with CD-ROM, graphical display and sound capability, matched to the speed of the CPU.
MS-DOS	*See* DOS
MSN	Microsoft Network. Microsoft's commercial on-line service.
navigator	Customized shell simplifying the approach to database exploration through menus.
NC	Network computer. A theoretical economical "blackbox" that connects directly to the Internet and is limited to that purpose.
netiquette	Guidelines for proper behavior in e-mail postings.
newsgroup	Usenet-administered public discussion on a dedicated topic. Similar to a bulletin board, conference, forum, and special interest groups within other organizations.
NIC	Network information center. Generic term for support facility for hosts and ISP computers.
NISO	National Information Standards Organization
node	A computer connected directly to Internet high-speed lines, as opposed to terminals and workstations.
NREN	National Research and Education Network, proposed in Congress as an extension of NSFnet, q.v.
NSF	National Science Foundation. Through NSFnet, it once funded a portion of the Internet.
NSFnet	The original backbone network on which the Internet was built. Established by NSF.
NTIS	National Technical Information Center, a Department of Commerce Agency
OCLC	(1) Online computer library catalog; (2) Online Computer Library Center, in Dublin, Ohio, the largest bibliographic database in the world.
OPAC	Online public access catalog

OSI	Open Systems Interconnection, a developing international network connection standard of ISO, q.v.
OS/2	Operating System/2, IBM's personal computer operating system.
packet	Basic unit of network information transfer, consisting of headers and data.
packet-switching	Means of network data transmission.
Perl	Unix-based programming language, often used in development of Internet applications.
PERT	Project evaluation and review technique
PIM	Personal information manager. Generic name for computer programs that track appointments, phone calls, other similar classes of information.
POP	Post-office Protocol, a method for handling e-mail.
PPP	Point-to-point protocol for dial-up packet-switching
PROFNET	Professors' Network
protocol	Rules governing communications between systems.
RAM	Random access memory
ROM	Read only memory
robot	Automated WWW searching program supplanted by more sophisticated spiders, q.v.
router	Network computer. Controls packet-switched traffic.
rtfm	Read the f_ manual (friendly, fuzzy, whatever).
server	Network-connected computer, providing resources to users.
shell	An interface between an operating system and its user.
SICI	Serial item and contribution identifier. A standardized code for classification of journals and periodicals.
SIG	Special interest group. *See also* newsgroup.

SIRIS	Smithsonian Institution Research Information System
SLIP	Serial line Internet protocol
SMTP	Simple mail transfer protocol, governing e-mail transmission.
sockets	The TCP/IP protocol stack.
spider	Highly automated WWW searching program that seeks and records new home pages, usually operated during off-peak hours to avoid exclusionary traffic.
SRE	Standard for Robot Exclusion. A set of rules permitting Web site owners to identify pages they do not want traversed by spiders.
SuDoc	Superintendent of Documents. Classification number assigned to U.S. government documents.
Sun	Unix-based, mid-range computer, product of Sun Microsystems Inc. Often an Internet host.
swais	Simple wide-area information server (see WAIS).
SYSOP	System operator, the administrator of a BBS or network server.
System-7	Apple's operating system for the Macintosh.
T1	Identifier of high speed, high bandwidth data communications facilities, operating in the order of two megabits per second.
TCP	Transmission control protocol to ensure correct transfer of data.
TCP/IP	Transmission Control Protocol/Internet Protocol, combination of formats and procedures governing data transfer between network-connected computers.
telnet	(1) Utility program for remote login; (2) command to initiate a remote connection.
TIA	(1) The Internet Adapter, client-server package allowing a shell account to operate under SLIP/PPP protocols; (2) e-mail short-speak, "thanks in advance."

Unix	Operating system developed by AT&T, now owned by Novell.
URL	Uniform resource locator, a fully qualified pathway to a directory or file on an Internet node.
UUCP	Unix-to-Unix Copy Program, commonly used as an e-mail collector.
Veronica	Resource locator developed at University of Nevada that searches through Gopher databases.
VM	Virtual machine. Identifies a specific type of IBM mainframe often serving the Internet.
VT-100	One of the most common terminal types, that has become a standard. Originally designed by Digital Equipment Corporation to connect to the VAX mid-range computer.
WAIS	Wide-Area Information Server, indexed database system
World Wide Web	Technology providing an interface for linking and presenting multimedia data across networks.
Windows	Microsoft's operating system
WWW	*See* World Wide Web
X25	CCITT standard for packet-switching
Z39.50	ANSI standard for the exchange of bibliographic information. Z39 generally indicates library standards.

Notes

I. Net Ready

1. National Commission on Libraries and Information Science (NCLIS), *The 1996 National Survey of Public Libraries and the Internet: Progress and Issues: Final Report*, by John Carlo Bertot, Charles R. McClure, and Douglas L. Zweizig.

   Available in print from NCLIS, 1110 Vermont Ave. Suite 820, Washington, DC 20005, and on the web at http://istweb.syr.edu/Project/Faculty/McClure-NSPL96/NSPL96_T.html
2. *New York Times*, May 7, 1997, Section D, 1:5; Forester Research, Inc.

4. Base Level Searches

1. "Information Retrieval Application Service Definition and Protocol Specification for Open Systems Interconnection," ANSI Z39.50, makes sure that diverse library systems can somehow communicate with each other.

5. Searching on the Internet

1. Newsgroup lists and their contents change often, and with use. The reader would not find the same display in alt.best.of.internet, from which this was captured.

2. The proper name of copyrighted material is capitalized here upon introduction. Acronyms or command versions of programs are shown as used in practice. Unix requires that program names, invoked as commands, be in lower case. Thus trn would be issued at the Unix prompt for the Threaded ReadNews program.

3. The term "home site" is introduced to differentiate between your service provider and other servers on the Internet. Telnet application programs sometimes use the term to inform you what is your currently active directory. Home site never refers to your personal computer, which is considered a "terminal" regardless of how it is connected.

4. The primary reason is that Gopher was developed at the University of Minnesota, in the Gopher state.

5. For several more, see the later referenced *New York Times, Cyber-Times Navigator*. Also read, John December with Neil Randall. *The World Wide Web Unleashed.* Indianapolis: Sams Publishing, 1994.

6. In terms of Web design, tools such as Gopher, and resources that are not written in html (contain no hypertext) are not part of the Web. (December and Randall, *op. cit.* page 322). Targets, in which you cannot go any further make up the edge of the World Wide Web. I'm inclined to use edge to mean the ultimate texts, and not the tools that get me there.

9. A Look Ahead

1. Would you like a map of Cambridge and environs? Check out Interactive Atlas at http://www.mapquest.com/

Bibliography

CD-ROMs

Most CD-ROMs are available through major retail and mail-order software suppliers. Some are advertised and can be purchased on the Web.

Encarta Multimedia Encyclopedia 98 (Microsoft), 30,000 entries; owners can arrange updates through a special Web site.

Encyclopaedia Britannica (Encyclopaedia Britannica, Inc.), full thirty volume source with graphics and hypertext searching.

Gale Directory of Databases. Kathleen Young Marcaccio, ed. (Detroit: Gale Research Inc., 1991). A merger of former reference books, Directory of Online Databases and Directory of Portable Databases, is now available on diskette, online, and CD-ROM. Call 800-347-4253 for information.

Global Explorer (DeLorme Mapping), 20,000 entries with street maps of 100 cities.

Grolier Multimedia Encyclopedia (Grolier), 5,000 entries based upon the twenty-one-volume *Academic American Encyclopedia*.

InfoTrac (Information Access Company), magazine index released monthly; accessible in many public libraries.

Mountain High Maps (Digital Wisdom, Inc.), world geographic information with some ability to manipulate it.

Microsoft Bookshelf (Microsoft), includes 15,000 entries in the Concise Columbia Encyclopedia, 100 maps in the Hammond Intermediate World Atlas, and short versions of *The American Heritage Dictionary, Roget's Thesaurus*, the *Concise Columbia Dictionary of Quotations*, and the *World Almanac and Book of Facts*.

Oxford English Reference Library (Oxford University Press), for use with DOS or OS/2 operating systems.

Random House Unabridged Electronic Dictionary (Random House), for Macintosh or IBM-compatible.

RedShift 2 (Maris Multimedia), astronomy via multimedia.

Periodicals

"Annals of Scholarship: Discards." Nicholson Baker. *The New Yorker*, 70, no. 7 (April 4, 1994): 64–86. Discusses in very negative terms the transition from library card catalogs to online services. This article is also included in Baker's collection of essays, *The Size of Thoughts: Essays and Other Lumber*. New York: Random House, 1996.

"Annals of Software: Byte Verse." Anthony Lane. *The New Yorker*, 71, no. 1 (February 1995): 102–17. Pricey poetry on CD-ROM.

Internet World Magazine (ISBN 1064-3923) lists ISPs; Mecklermedia Corporation, 11 Ferry Lane West, Westport, CT 06880.

"The 1996 National Survey of Public Libraries and the Internet: Progress and Issues: Final Report." John Carlo Bertot, Charles R. McClure, and Douglas L. Zweizig. National Commission on Libraries and Information Science (NCLIS). Available in print from NCLIS, 1110 Vermont Ave. Suite 820, Washington, D.C. 20005, and on the web at http://istweb.syr.edu/Project/Faculty/McClure-NSPL96/NSPL96_T.html

"The Web Untangled." Rick Ayre and Kevin Reichard. *PC Magazine* 14, no. 3 (February 1995): 173–96.

Reference Manuals

Any library should have a large collection of reference publications. Sequenced here by title with credit to authors, editors and compilers, is a representative sample of those we have found useful.

American Library Directory, 1996–97. 49th ed. 2 vol. New Providence, NJ: R.R. Bowker, 1996. Lists most libraries in the nation, the size of their collections and descriptions of special holdings; not indexed by subject. For subject index refer to Lee Ash's *Subject Collections.*

Second Barnhart Dictionary of New English, The. Clarence L. Barnhart, Sol Steinmetz, Robert K. Barnhart, eds. Bronxville, NY: Barnhart Books, 1980.

Books in Print. Annual. New Providence, NJ: R. R. Bowker. A multivolume directory listing current American books by author and by subject. See also *Forthcoming Books.*

Chicago Manual of Style, The. 14th ed. Chicago: University of Chicago Press, 1993.

Concise Dictionary of American Biography. 3rd ed. New York: Scribner, 1980.

Directories in Print: 1995. Terri Kessler Schell, ed. Detroit: Gale Research Inc., 1994.

Directory of Directories on the Internet: A Guide to Information Sources. Gregory Newby. Westport, CN: Meckler Publishing, 1994.

Encyclopedia of Associations: 1995. Carol A. Schwartz and Rebecca L. Turner, eds. Detroit: Gale Research Inc., 1994.

Facts on File. New York: Facts on File, Inc. Weekly digest of world news, loose-leaf bound, extracted from major periodicals; includes cumulative index.

Forthcoming Books, supplement to the *Books in Print Subject Guide.* New Providence, NJ: R. R. Bowker. Semimonthly.

Government CD-ROMs: A Practical Guide to Searching Electronic Databases. John Maxymuk, editor. Westport, CN: Mecklermedia, 1994. Appendix contains annotated list of GPO CD-ROMS.

Guide to Holdings of the Still Picture Branch of the National Archives. Washington, DC: National Archives and Records Administration, 1995.

Guide to the National Archives of the United States. 3 vol. Washington, DC: National Archives and Records Administration, 1995.

Guide to Reference Books. 11th ed. Robert Balay, ed. Vee Friesner Carrington, associate ed. Chicago, American Library Association, 1996.

Internet Compendium. Louis Rosenfeld, Joseph Janes, and Martha Vander Holk, comps. 3 vols. New York: Neal-Schuman Publishers, Inc., 1995. Health and science, social sciences, humanities.

Internet Directory, The. Eric Braun with Mark Leger, New York: Fawcett Columbine, 1996. OPACs and many other Internet resources.

Modem USA. Lynn Motley, Takoma Park, MD: Allium Press, 1994. Bulletin board systems, addresses and phone numbers.

National Trade and Professional Associations of the United States: 1995. Washington, D.C.: Columbia Books, 1995.

New Columbia Encyclopedia. William H. Harris and Judith S. Levey, eds. New York, Columbia University Press, 1975.

New Encyclopaedia Britannica, The. 15th ed. 32 vols. Chicago: Encyclopaedia Britannica, 1995.

New York Times Index, The. New York: The New York Times Company. (Annual since 1851); current year, quarterly.

New York Public Library Desk Reference, The. New York: Macmillan, 1995.

1995 Information Industry Directory. Annette Novallo, ed. 2 vol. Detroit: Gale Research, Inc., 1995. Start with this set, and use it as a base reference.

Official Museum Directory, 1997, The. 2 vols. New Providence, NJ: R. R. Bowker. Annual.

On Internet: An International Title and Subject Guide to Electronic Journals, Newsletters, Books and Discussion Lists on the Internet, Westport, CN: Meckler Publishing. Annual.

OPAC Directory 1993. Rega, Regina, comp. Westport, CN: Meckler Publishing, 1993. Look for latest edition.

Reader's Guide to Periodical Literature. New York: H. W. Wilson. Available in print, on CD-ROM, and online. Some full-text. Published semi-monthly.

Search Sheets for OPACs on the Internet. Marcia Henry, Linda Keenan, and Michael Reagan. Westport, CN: Meckler Publishing, 1992.

Subject Collections. Lee Ash and Denis Lorenz, comps. New York: R. R. Bowker, 1967. Special book collections reported by academic, public and special libraries. See also *American Library Directory.*

Timetables of American History. Laurence Urdang, ed. New York: Simon & Schuster, 1981. Like Ferrell's *The Twentieth Century—An Almanac,* it puts history in a popular format for easy reference. Similarly, more recent books may be found in the same reference area.

Twentieth Century—An Almanac, The. Robert H. Ferrell, ed. New York: World Almanac Publications, 1984. History in easily readable format. More current sources may be available.

Webster's New Biographical Dictionary. Springfield, MA: Merriam-Webster, 1983.

Who's Who in America: 1997. 51st ed., 3 vol. New Providence, NJ: Marquis Who's Who, 1996.

Yearbook of Experts, Authorities and Spokespersons, An Encyclopedia of Sources. Washington, DC: Broadcast Interview Source. Annual.

Texts

Basbanes, Nicholas A., *Gentle Madness—Bibliophiles, Bibliomanes, and the Eternal Passion for Books, A.* New York: Henry Holt and Company, 1995. Fascinating reading about and for book collectors.

Burack, Sylvia K., editor. *The Writer's Handbook.* Boston: The Writer Inc, 1995.

December, John, and Neil Randall. *World Wide Web Unleashed, The.* Indianapolis: Sams Publishing, 1994. Look for the latest edition; things change rapidly.

Dern, Daniel P. *Internet Guide for New Users, The.* New York: McGraw-Hill, Inc., 1995.

Gibaldi, Joseph. *MLA Handbook for Writers of Research Papers.* 4th ed. New York: Modern Language Association of America, 1997.

Goldmann, Nahum. *Online Information Hunting.* Blue Ridge Summit, PA: TAB Books, 1992.

Hahn, Harley, and Rick Stout. *Internet Complete Reference, The.* New York: McGraw-Hill, 1995.

————. *Internet Yellow Pages, The.* New York: McGraw-Hill, 1995.

Harris, Sherwood, editor. *New York Public Library Book of How and Where to Look It Up, The.* New York: Prentice Hall, 1991.

Holman, Sona, and Lillian Friedman. *How to Lie About Your Age.* New York: Collier Books, 1979. Out-of-print paperback, but good for a laugh if available. Mid-century social history.

Krol, Ed. *Whole Internet User's Guide and Catalog, Second Edition, The.* Sebastopol, CA: O'Reilly & Associates, 1994. Outdated, but the guidance remains useful.

Lesko, Matthew. *Lesko's Info-Power.* Detroit: Visible Ink Press, 1994.

Levine, John R., and Carol Baroudi. *Internet for Dummies.* 2nd Ed. San Mateo, CA: IDG Books Worldwide Inc., 1994.

Li, Xia, and Nancy B. Crane. *Electronic Style: A Guide to Citing Electronic Information.* Westport, CN: Meckler, 1993.

Mann, Thomas. *Library Reference Models.* New York: Oxford University Press, 1993.

McClure, Charles R., William E. Moen, and Joe Ryan, eds. *Libraries and* the Internet/NREN: Perspectives, Issues and Challenges. Westport, CN: Mecklermedia, 1994.

Parco, Vincent. *Researching Public Records: How to Get Anything on Anybody.* Seacaucus, NJ: Carol Publishing Group, 1994. Paperback guide to being a "private eye."

Robinson, Judith Schiek. *Tapping the Government Grapevine.* Phoenix, AZ: Oryx Press, 1993. Explanation of the federal government's internal channels.

Schumacher, Michael. *Creative Conversations: The Writer's Complete Guide to Conducting Interviews.* Cincinnati: Writer's Digest Books, 1990.

Whitely, Sandy, ed. *American Library Association Research Handbook: An Information Age Guide to Researching Facts and Topics.* New York: Random House, 1994.

Index